letters to a young
evangelical

Tony Campolo

letters to a young evangelical

BASIC
BOOKS

A Member of the Perseus Books Group
New York

Copyright © 2006 by Tony Campolo

Published by Basic Books

A Member of the Perseus Books Group

Cataloging-in-Publication information for this book is available from
the Library of Congress.

0-465-00831-3

978-0-465-00831-5

Basic Books are available at special discounts for bulk purchases in
the U.S. by corporations, institutions, and other organizations. For
more information, please contact the Special Markets Department at
special.markets@perseusbooks.com.

10 9 8 7 6 5 4 3 2 1

Contents

Contents

▇ Acknowledgments

A book like this requires some thank-yous. In putting these letters together, I was very dependent on Christin Fenton and Sarah Blaisdell, who did the typing; my nephew, Doug Davidson, who proofread what I wrote; and Lara Heimert, who edited this book and gave it a semblance of order and intellectual consistency. A special thanks goes to my personal assistant, James Warren, who coordinated all the efforts required to get this book into print. I offer them my heartfelt gratitude.

A word of thanks goes to Eastern University, where I did my undergraduate studies and where I've taught sociology for almost thirty-nine years. This Evangelical institution has provided me with colleagues who have done much to help me develop my worldview, and with a president, Dr. David Black, who has encouraged me and defended me against my critics. Most of all, Eastern has given me the opportunity to share in the lives of truly amazing students. Some of them not only listened to

ments

what I had to say, but went on to live out the Evangelical faith with radical commitment. I hope and pray that this book honors them.

viii

Introduction:
Why These Letters?

Writing letters to young Christians is nothing new. Almost twenty centuries ago, the apostle Paul did it. He wrote to Timothy, his protégé, with the hope that his letters would guide this fledgling Christian missionary and inspire him to realize his potential as an evangelist and church leader. Paul's epistles to Timothy have come down to us as part of the New Testament, and they are jam-packed with good theology and wise council.

Paul wrote to Timothy for many of the same reasons that motivate me to write to young Evangelicals today. He wanted to keep Timothy from being swept up in movements within the church that distorted the Gospel and justified destructive behavior. Knowing that young people can be easily seduced by fast-talking sophisticates who construct false images of Christ, Paul wanted to keep Timothy orthodox (2 Corinthians 11:12–14). Paul wanted this promising novice at church leadership to develop intellectually so that he would be prepared to relate the Gospel message effectively to those outside the Christian community as well as those within it (2 Timothy 2:15). Most important, Paul wanted Timothy to develop the kind of spiritual disciplines that would nurture him into Christian maturity.

Imitating Paul, I will address the letters in this book to an imagined young Evangelical named Timothy. My hope is that these letters might provide young readers in today's world something like the helpful advice and instruction that Paul gave to his Timothy many years ago.

Each of these letters will also be addressed to an imagined young woman named Junia, because young women are just as important to us as young men. I am convinced that Paul would have had no objection to my approach, especially since he had no problem with women holding key roles of leadership. In Romans 16:7, Paul recognized Junia, a woman, as a fellow apostle—the supreme role for a preacher and teacher in ecclesiastical rankings.

It always amazes me to see the lengths to which some of my Evangelical brothers and sisters are willing to go in concealing the fact that women held prominent leadership roles in the early church. They even seem ready to change the Bible if it runs contrary to the belief that only men should hold high offices in Christendom. When certain Evangelicals produced their own translation of the Scriptures in the first edition of the New International Version, they changed the name Junia to

Junius—a man's name. You may come to your own conclusions as to why they did that, but I think it was an attempt to restructure the Bible to legitimate their own chauvinist ideas about who should be eligible to lead the church. In an effort to restore Junia to her true role within the history of the church, I have chosen to address these letters to her as well as to Timothy.

One of my biggest concerns about American Evangelicalism today is that, in the minds of many, it has become synonymous with the Religious Right. Given that most of our prominent leaders and their followers have been the base of the most conservative wing of the Republican Party, it is easy to see why those outside our community perceive us that way.

Those on the Religious Right have the microphone. Their voices are the ones heard on thousands of religious radio and television shows. They are the ones quoted by the secular media as speaking for us. But I want our modern-day Timothys and Junias to know that there is a significant minority within the Evangelical community that embraces progressive politics. In fact, if the issues of abortion and homosexual marriage were set aside, Evangelicals would split right down the middle politically, with half of us voting Democratic and the other half Republican.

I don't want to give the impression that I think there is anything wrong with Christians being Republicans. In reality, Christians on both sides of the political aisle are committed to many of the same values. I believe that Christians on the political right are just as eager as those on the left to help the poor, bring peace to the world, rescue the environment from degradation, and overcome racism. Working for social justice is not a prerogative of the left.

What differentiates Evangelicals on the right from those on the left are the different ways each group proposes to achieve social justice. Those on the right tend to put their trust in the private sector (e.g., churches and other charitable organizations) to meet the needs of the poor and oppressed, whereas those on the left believe that the government must play a major role in solving social problems.

When it comes to social ministries, those on the Religious Right excel in financial support and volunteerism. They are always among the first to come to the aid of victims after a disaster such as Hurricane Katrina. The volunteers recruited by Pat Robertson deserve praise for their work among the poor. Likewise, the ministries of Samaritan's Purse, an organization long guided by Billy Graham's son, Franklin Graham, deserve great credit for providing medical services and feeding programs to people in Third World countries.

As commendable as these ministries are, however, many of us believe that something more is needed. I, along with many other Evangelicals who are not part of the Religious Right, believe that Christians should engage in efforts to change the political and economic structures of our society because these structures do not adequately address the needs of the poor and oppressed. In fact, prevailing social structures are often responsible for much of their misery.

We believe that churches alone cannot provide health care for the 44 million Americans who have none; government must step in to help meet this need. Private charities cannot compensate the working poor, who are growing poorer in real terms every day because, despite significant inflation, their minimum wage has not been raised in a decade.

The businesses and industries of America, which have made profits their raison d'être, are not likely to look out for the public good unless required to do so by law. Government controls are needed.

We believe in challenging a government that sets aside less than four-tenths of 1 percent of its federal budget to help the poor worldwide while spending hundreds of billions on the military and on boondoggles that serve little more than the political interests of the legislators who sponsor them.

In many cases, we believe in policies and programs that put us in direct opposition to more conservative Evangelicals. For instance, many conservative Evangelicals decry public education because they believe that our schools are teaching children secular humanism. In contrast, we believe in working to increase funding to those schools, usually in poor neighborhoods, that are underfunded and therefore underserving their students.

When it comes to protecting the environment, the Religious Right questions whether there is even a problem to be addressed. We believe that there is.

On a host of other issues as well—from homosexuality to the war in Iraq—there is a much broader range of opinion within the Evangelical community than you might think. I will be writing to you about many of these issues in this book, and I encourage you to keep your minds open to the wide variety of ways that Evangelicals can approach all of these issues.

Those of us within the Evangelical community who embrace a progressive political agenda are often referred to in the media as the Evangelical Left. We don't like that designation because it suggests that we are an arm of the Democratic Party in the same way in which the Religious Right has become an arm of the Republican Party. We contend that to ally Jesus with either political party is idolatry. The Jesus of Scripture will not conform to the ideologies of any party. He stands in judgment of all of our political agendas and calls Christians in each and every party to examine their respective party platforms in accord with his teachings.

Some people have referred to us as progressive Evangelicals. We also shy away from that designation for a variety of reasons, not the least of which is that the term *Evangelical* carries with it a great deal of baggage. The word *Evangelical* is accurate and useful to describe our theology. But in the outside world, it is too often confused with *the Religious Right*, which has effectively appropriated the word for its own purposes.

These confusions led a group of us who are Evangelical writers and speakers to try to come up with some other designation. After much discussion, we enthusiastically decided to call ourselves Red-Letter Christians. Strangely enough, this name was suggested to us by a secular Jewish country-and-western disc jockey in Nashville, Tennessee. When he heard about our intense desire to be faithful to the words of Jesus as recorded in the New Testament, he said, "Oh! You folks are into those verses in the Bible that are in red letters!" Of course, he was referring to the old King James Version Bibles that had all the words of Jesus printed in red.

While I will refer to "Evangelicals" throughout the letters that follow, and define myself as one of them, do be aware that the social values that I will be expressing make me part of the socially and politically progressive minority within Evangelicalism increasingly known as Red-Letter Christians.

Let me warn you right up front that if you try to live out the teachings described in the red letters of the New Testament, you may well be viewed as a radical. After all, they didn't put Jesus on a cross for saying nice things that people in the ruling religious, political, and economic establishment wanted to hear. His teachings, as recorded in the red letters of Scripture, were so threatening to the status quo that religious leaders believed that the survival of their entire social system—the system that had given them so much wealth, power, and prestige—was contingent on Jesus's execution (John 11:49–50).

The red letters of the New Testament challenge us still. As I will explain in these letters, the teachings of Jesus run contrary to many of our current policies, lifestyles, and beliefs. The red letters challenge Americans' justifications for accumulating wealth, support of capital punishment, ready endorsement of war, rampant consumerism, rebellion against sexual prohibitions that have sustained purity and modesty for generations, and arrogant use of economic power to fulfill national self-interests to the detriment of other nations.

Some will accuse me of radicalizing Jesus by distorting his message. I am constantly reflecting on that judgment, trying to figure out whether that criticism is valid. But I contend that a true and careful reading of the red letters in the New Testament can radicalize any honest reader—and I try to be honest. I encourage you to judge for yourselves whether the positions I take on controversial issues are true to the red letters.

1

■ Welcome!

Dear Timothy and Junia,

Welcome to the Evangelical world!

The Evangelical world is very different now than it was when I was growing up a half century ago. Back then, we Evangelicals were little more than a small blip on the radar screens of those surveying the U.S. religious landscape. In those days, mainline denominations dominated American religion, and many of their leaders viewed us, with condescension, as a reactionary sect lacking what they called "relevancy to the modern world." Images of the Scopes trial—during which William Jennings Bryan defended Fundamentalists' belief in a six-day creation—loomed large in their memories.

Over the course of the twentieth century, Western societies came to believe that "truth" could only be proved according to scientific criteria. Evangelical beliefs, marked by miraculous events such as a virgin birth, resurrections from the dead, and a Savior who walked on water, did not fare well in that environment. Sophisticated intellectuals dismissed us because we refused to accept the arguments of modernist biblical scholars who raised questions about the historical validity of Scripture and claimed that the Bible was just a collection of religious myths and metaphorical accounts of history.

As the sociologist Peter Berger explained in his 1967 book, *The Sacred Canopy*, the West had severed itself from an ancient, magical form of religiosity and replaced it with a modern worldview in which religion was reduced to that which is rational and ethical. Berger and others believed that this drive toward rationalization was irreversible, and that for religion to remain relevant (there's that word again), it would have to adapt to the canons of modernity.

During those days, we Evangelicals established a fortress mentality and concentrated on defending ourselves against the onslaught of liberal theology. Many young people, believing in the supremacy of scientific thinking, deserted our churches, scoffed at our messages, and refused to accept any doctrine that seemed to defy their rationalistic ways of thinking. At the convocations of the mainline denominations to which most Christians belonged in those days, Fundamentalism was regularly ridiculed. The colleges and universities established by mainline denominations were rapidly secularized, and the religious commitments that had given them birth were held in derision. The popular media, taking its cue from Sinclair Lewis's *Elmer Gantry*, made evangelists out to be charlatans. In those days, we Evangelicals were somewhat apologetic when explaining to outsiders who we were and what we believed.

Berger and other "modernists" could not have imagined what would happen to American religion by the end of the twentieth century. Those who are still with us from those days can only gasp at the resurgence of Evangelicalism and the ways in which this movement has gained the prestige and power it presently enjoys. As presidential candidates vie with each other to try to convince the 55 million Americans claiming to be "born again" that they, too, are religious, liberal thinkers look on with disbelief that the world has changed so quickly.

Martin Marty, an eminent religious scholar, has said that Evangelicalism has so effectively ended the hegemony that mainline denominations once exercised over contemporary Protestantism that the latter should really be referred to as "the sidelined denominations." Every year, just about every mainline denomination registers significant declines in membership, while many independent Evangelical churches show dramatic increases. The few mainline denominational churches that do grow are often churches that have espoused Evangelical styles of preaching and worship. Many of these churches find the denominational labels affixed to their outdoor display signs to be more of a hindrance than an asset in attracting members.

How did we come so far, so fast? One of the primary reasons is the evangelist Billy Graham. An icon of our movement, Graham is the closest thing we Evangelical Protestants have to a pope. He has served us well, expressing and demonstrating what is best about us in so many different ways. Graham's preaching has been exemplary; the fiscal accountability of his organization has been impeccable; and the way he has presented himself in the media—from *The Tonight Show* to *Larry King Live*—has made us proud. For the most part, Billy Graham has given the impression that Evangelicals can be reasonable, kind, nonjudgmental, and politically nonpartisan—which is more than can be said for many television evangelists.

Just after World War II, Billy Graham, a recent graduate of Wheaton College in Illinois, along with some friends, formed Youth for Christ, an organization committed to evangelizing the young people of America. However, Graham earned widespread public attention only after newspaper magnate William Randolph Hearst heard Graham in Los Angeles early in his preaching career and gave word to his network of editors that this young evangelist was something special. After that, Graham was front-page news everywhere, and the publicity helped him attract ever-increasing audiences.

I first heard Billy Graham speak in 1957, at the old Madison Square Garden in New York City. At the time, I was a twenty-three-year-old pastor of two small churches in New Jersey. I had brought a busload of my church members to the big city to hear this newly famous preacher. There was not a vacant seat in the building.

I sat in awe as Graham called upon the urban people of Gotham City to repent of their sins and surrender their lives to Christ. Charisma is hard to define, but it's easy to recognize it when you see it—and I saw it that night. Holding a huge Bible plopped open in one hand and strongly gesturing to the audience with a pointed finger of the other, Graham communicated an urgency in his message that held us in rapt attention.

As he wrapped up his sermon, the great evangelist invited all who wanted to be "born again" to come forward and stand in the open space in front of the preaching platform. It looked as though more than a thousand people responded to his invitation. A mass choir of several hundred singers from churches throughout the New York metropolitan area sang as the people came forward. I still remember their singing the standard invitation hymn of Evangelicals:

> *Just as I am, without one plea*
> *But that Thy blood was shed for me,*
> *And that Thou bid'st me come to Thee,*
> *O Lamb of God, I come, I come!*

Hundreds of carefully trained counselors were waiting for those who streamed down the aisles of that vast sports arena. These counselors were more than ready to pray for the would-be converts, to give them tracts with helpful guidelines for the spiritual journey upon which they were embarking, and to gather personal information so that each of them could be referred to a local church that would nurture them into mature Christian lives.

The whole event was brilliantly organized—from the publicity and organizational work that drew the crowd to the orchestrated singing to the preaching and praying with those who made decisions for Christ. But the careful planning and organizational efficiency were not the most important elements of what transpired that night. No one present could deny the special charisma possessed by the preacher. Billy Graham had something special about him that seemed to come from beyond and above. Pentecostal Christians would say he had a "special anointing from the Lord."

If you carefully considered the words of Graham's sermon that night, you might have found them interesting but not especially profound. His message was a rather simple explanation of what a person must believe and do in order to be "born again." Of course, Graham's delivery was dynamic, and his good looks and head of shiny blond hair added to the impact he made from the pulpit that night. But all of those positive assets did not explain his incredible effectiveness. It was easy for me to believe that God's spirit was alive and working through Billy Graham as he spoke. There was a sense that some supernatural force controlled him—and it was this meta-physical force that drew his audience not so much to him but to the Jesus he preached.

We cannot know for certain how much of Evangelicalism's growing success and popularity over the next half century was determined by the preaching crusades Billy Graham conducted as he carried the Gospel around the world. But there is no doubt that his impact has been enormous—not only because of his own work, but also through the thousands of young preachers who learned from him and imitated his style. His rapid-fire preaching and his constant use of the phrase *the Bible says* to legitimate every point of his messages became almost standard fare among evangelists and remain so right down to our present day. These imitators accomplished great things, but, in the end, they were no match for the man who had inspired them. Without a doubt, Billy Graham preached the Gospel to more people than any other person in human history, and it's doubtful that we shall ever see the likes of him again.

Billy Graham showed the world that the heart of the Evangelical movement is our intensive zeal for "winning people to Christ." He made clear his belief that Jesus Christ is the only one who can deliver people from the punishing consequences of their sins and offer the promise of eternal life when this earthly life is over.

Those who were not possessed by the spiritual presence of Christ, Graham claimed, would be lost souls for time and eternity.

Because he truly loved people and did not want them to be lost, Graham urgently wanted to tell the salvation story as often and to as many people as possible. Graham did not attempt to play God by offering judgments about who was saved and who was lost, but he never backed off from his conviction that whoever was saved was saved through the sacrificial death of Christ on Calvary's cross. Graham's drive was the drive of all Evangelicals: to "rescue the perishing and care for the dying," as the old hymn goes. Whenever you find us, you will encounter Christians who want to make sure that your salvation is sealed by your belief in what Jesus did for you on the cross.

The zeal and urgency Graham brought to the Evangelical movement transformed the movement from within. It is this zeal, and our sense of urgency to save the lost, that has been responsible for the phenomenal growth of our churches. Most members of mainline churches are more hesitant to share their faith, and often consider it poor manners to bring up religion in friendly conversations at social gatherings. But we Evangelicals feel obligated to witness for Christ whenever we get the opportunity. Undoubtedly, sometimes we can be obnoxious in our constant efforts to squeeze in some testimony about what we believe, even when it might appear completely inappropriate. But there can be no question that we are generating results. We really do win converts through our incessant witnessing about what Christ has done and is doing in our lives. New converts are regularly joining our churches and swelling the memberships of our congregations, while the congregations of mainline churches are shrinking.

One of the most well-known mega-churches created through the outreach efforts of Evangelicals is the great Willow Creek Community Church in Barrington, Illinois. This particular church deserves special mention because its style of worship and its methods for bringing in new members have been imitated by other churches not only across America, but also around the world.

The format of Sunday services at Willow Creek Community Church is somewhat similar to what might be viewed on one of those late-night TV talk shows. The well-orchestrated program is built around a carefully selected theme. It includes skits that drive home pointed messages, well-performed music, and a twenty-minute talk in which the pastor uses interesting stories to illustrate his message. That the hour-long program is good entertainment does not mean that the meaningful truths it is designed to communicate are concealed.

When it comes to promotional techniques, the Willow Creek Community Church early on learned to use the Internet to connect with people throughout the greater Chicago area and draw them into the fellowship of the church. But more than anything else, the members of the congregation have learned that it is their responsibility to bring their friends, neighbors, and work associates to experience what the church has to offer.

A few years ago, members of this congregation celebrated their church's twenty-fifth anniversary. Bill Hybels, the founder and pastor of the church, wanted all who regularly attend any of its weekly services to gather together in one place at one time. Because more than 25,000 people attend Willow Creek services each week, the church rented the United Center in downtown Chicago for the celebration.

When the Willow Creek people came into that huge sports arena on the big night, each of them was given a small flashlight. Then, at a particular point in the evening program, the house lights were turned off. Pastor Hybels asked those who had had no previous church affiliation before coming to Willow Creek Community Church to turn on their flashlights and wave them over their heads. The results were amazing! Thousands upon thousands of flashlights were turned on. All sides of the center were ablaze with waving points of light. These lights, for the most part, represented converts who had been led to Christ through the zealous efforts of other Willow Creek Community Church members. Those shining lights were evidence of how effectively Evangelicals do evangelism.

While I've given you a peek at what we Evangelicals do and what makes us tick, I've not yet carefully defined just what we believe and what makes those beliefs distinctive. But this letter is long enough, so I'll have to wait for my next letter to spell out those things. For now, let me sign off by saying, "Stay alive in Christ."

Sincerely,
Tony

2

■ The Gospel According to Us

Dear Junia and Timothy,

As you may know, most Evangelicals at some point
make a decision to trust in Jesus for salvation and commit to becoming the kind of people he wants us to be. I
would like to spell out in more detail what this means
and offer some explanation of our basic doctrines and
what makes us distinctive.

First, however, it is important to explain that the very
word *Evangelical* is complicated these days because it en-
compasses such varied groups. For instance, most Pentecostals (who believe in glossolalia, or speaking in
tongues) call themselves Evangelicals. Yet some Southern Baptists who also claim the term think that people
who speak in tongues are "off the wall" and have been
carried away emotionally—or worse. Some Evangelicals
believe in "the rapture"—that is, that when Jesus returns, as he promised to, all true believers will be spir-
ited away from the earth to join him somewhere in the

sky. Other Evangelicals believe that in the Second Coming, Christ will return to Earth, join up with those of us who are working for God's kingdom here, and carry us to victory over the forces of evil that are so evident in our fallen world.

Some Evangelicals are extreme Calvinists who believe that God controls everything in the world in accord with what was predestined before the universe was spoken into existence. Still others hold to Wesleyan Arminianism, a theology that emphasizes free will and affirms "the openness of God"—the idea that God can change plans from time to time.

Some of us think that to be Evangelical is to be Republican and to embrace the ideology of the Religious Right. But there are others of us—a minority, to be sure—who espouse a liberal social and political agenda.

Critics of our movement sometimes claim that the term *Evangelical* is so amorphous that it has little specific meaning. I disagree. I believe that there are defining beliefs and commitments that Evangelicals hold in common and that render us cohesive despite our many differences.

Evangelicals are distinct from other Christians in several important ways. First, to be an Evangelical is to believe certain things—specifically, the doctrines clearly stated in the Apostles' Creed. This centuries-old statement of faith sums up those essential beliefs that we affirm to be literally true. The Apostles' Creed has been recited in churches down through the ages, but I'll state it here in case you aren't familiar with it:

> *I believe in God the Father Almighty, maker of heaven and earth; and in Jesus Christ His only Son our Lord; who was conceived by the Holy Ghost; born of the Virgin Mary; suffered under Pontius Pilate; was crucified, dead, and buried; He descended into hell; the third day He rose again from the dead; He ascended into heaven; and sitteth on the right hand of God the Father Almighty; from thence He shall come to judge the quick and the dead. I believe in the Holy Ghost; the holy catholic* church; the communion of saints; the forgiveness of sins; the resurrection of the body; and the life everlasting.*

Second, Evangelicals have a very high view of Scripture. We believe that these writings were divinely inspired. By that, we mean that when the authors of these Scriptures sat down to write, the Holy Spirit—that third member of the Trinity—mystically and miraculously guided what they penned. We believe that these authors were so fully under the influence of God as they wrote that their writings became an "infallible guide for faith and practice."

Some Evangelicals go beyond calling the Scriptures an infallible guide for what we should believe and how

---

*Catholic, here, means *universal*.

we should live our lives, and argue that they are inerrant. By that, they mean that the setting down on parchment of every word of the Holy Writ was so governed by the Holy Spirit that there is not a single mistake or theological error in the words recorded. There are sophisticated professors of theology, such as my good friend, the well-known author Ron Sider, who are certain that the original manuscripts were inerrant, even if they concede that mistakes might have crept into these writings as they were transcribed by hand and passed on from one generation to the next. These Evangelical scholars claim that whatever mistakes might have crept in at the hands of scribes are negligible.

Personally, I think the question of the inerrancy of the original manuscripts is irrelevant because the originals are not available to us. All Evangelicals say that, whatever may be the shortcomings of the copies of Scripture that have come down to us through history, there is little doubt that they contain essential truths we need to know to believe in Christ and live out his will. When preaching or teaching, we Evangelicals always use the Scriptures to validate what we have to say. Any ideas articulated by our church leaders, and any moral principles preached from our pulpits, must be in harmony with what is written in Scripture to be acceptable to those of us who sit in the pews.

The third and most important characteristic that distinguishes Evangelicals from other Christians is the

ultimate significance we place on having a personal, intimate, and transforming relationship with the resurrected
and living Jesus Christ. We Evangelicals have no doubt
that the same Jesus who, in the words of the Apostles'
Creed, "suffered under Pontius Pilate; was crucified,
dead, and buried ... [and on] the third day rose again
from the dead" is alive and personally present in the
world today. We believe that he waits to be invited into
an intimate relationship with anyone who will prayerfully surrender to him.

Even as I write to you right now, I am aware of the
presence of Jesus Christ around me and in me. Day by day,
this ever-present, living Christ is in relationship with me,
and this interactive relationship has transforming effects in
my life. Becoming a completely actualized Christian is, for
me, an ongoing process. While I am not yet what I should
be or would be, I am also not what I once was. My favorite
passage of Scripture is Philippians 3:13–14:

> I have not reached perfection; I do not claim to have
> hold of it yet. What I do say is this: Forgetting what is
> behind and straining towards what lies ahead, I press
> towards the finish line, to win the prize to which God
> has called me in Jesus Christ.

It is clear in this passage that the apostle Paul, who
wrote these words, was involved in the same kind of de-
velopmental process I am trying to describe.

Jesus does not speak to me in words, but when I stop and pay attention, I become very aware of his presence. He is a prodding influence, urging me to do things in new ways and to embrace new attitudes—and this makes me, little by little, more of the person Christ wants me to be.

We surrender our lives and allow Christ's spirit to saturate us with his presence and transform us—this is what it means to be "born again." Some Evangelicals are initiated into this born-again relationship with Christ in the context of a dramatic crisis in their lives. Consequently, they can point to particular dates and times when Christ "saved" them. When I was a boy growing up in a lower-middle-class neighborhood in West Philadelphia, my mother, a convert to Evangelical Christianity from a Catholic Italian immigrant family, hoped I would have one of those dramatic "born again" experiences. That was the way in which she had come into a personal relationship with Christ. She took me to hear one evangelist after another, praying that I would go to the altar and come away "converted." But it never worked for me. I would go down the aisle as the people around me sang what was called "the invitation hymn," but I just didn't feel as if anything happened to me. For a while I despaired, wondering whether I would ever get "saved." It took me quite some time to realize that entering into a personal relationship with Christ does not always happen that way.

In my case, intimacy with Christ has developed gradually over the years, primarily through what Catholic mystics call "centering prayer." Each morning, as soon as I wake up, I take time—sometimes as much as a half hour—to center myself on Jesus. I say his name over and over again to drive back the 101 things that begin to clutter up my mind the minute I open my eyes. Jesus is my mantra, as some would say. The constant repetition of his name clears my head of everything but the awareness of his presence. By driving back all other concerns, I am able to create what the ancient Celtic Christians called "the thin place." The thin place is that spiritual condition wherein the separation between the self and God becomes so thin that God is able to break through and envelop the soul.

There's an old African American spiritual that goes, "Woke up this morning with my mind stayed on Jesus." That perfectly describes what I do in the morning. After a while, an inner stillness pervades my whole being, and in that quietude I begin to feel myself being invaded by the spirit of Jesus Christ—and certainty and joy fill my soul.

I'm not sure what will work for you, but having an ongoing sense of an interactive relationship with the living Jesus is at the core of what it means to be an Evangelical. There is no one way to establish the love relationship with the One who is, as we say, "the only way." What is important is that you find your own way of seeking and maintaining intimacy with Jesus. Without it, you'll be spiritually dead.

Sincerely,
Tony

3

▉ Becoming Actualized Christians

Dear Timothy and Junia,

Having an intimate relationship with Christ is at the core of being an Evangelical. To this end, I want to urge you to consider three things. They are:

Centering prayer

Contemplative Bible study

An accountability group that helps you maintain spiritual disciplines for consistent Christian living

Allow me to explain what is involved in each of these and how you might go about making them part of your life.

As I made clear in my last letter, all spiritual development begins with prayer. Most Christians think that there's not much involved in the art of praying—you just tell God what you need and want. Regrettably, most of us never get beyond that kind of praying. Too many of us continue to think of prayer as my son did at age seven, when he came into the living room one evening and said, "I'm going to bed! I'm going to be praying! Does anybody want anything?"

It's all right to make your requests known to God. The Bible tells us to do that. Furthermore, the Bible tells us, "You have not because you ask not" (James 4:2). But praying should be more than simply presenting a list of nonnegotiable demands to the Almighty. Two thousand years ago, the Disciples asked Jesus what this something more might be and how they should pray. Jesus told them that when they pray, they should go into a closet, shut the door, and pray to God in secret (Matthew 6:6). I won't tell you that you should literally go into a closet—but if you are going to pray in depth, you ought to do something like that. You should go somewhere where there are no distractions.

When I was a child at church camp, my cabin counselor told me to go out on a hillside, surrounded by nature's beauty, and meditate upon Jesus. That never worked for me. There were too many distractions in nature. I would notice the birds and the sky and the grass. The sounds of living creatures would seduce me into listening to them, and soon the conscious awareness of God was gone.

I need solitude and darkness to concentrate upon God, so going into a closet isn't such a bad idea for me.

However, closing my eyes while sitting in a quiet place will usually do just as well. I try to do my praying in the morning. I get up about a half hour before I have to, and I "center down" on Jesus. As I lie alone in bed in the early-morning quiet, I wait for God to invade me, to fill my soul, and to take possession of me.

I wish I could say it always happens. To be frank, on most mornings nothing happens. Nothing of God is felt, but I keep at it because I never know when the Spirit will take hold of me. Jesus once said that the Spirit is like the wind, which "blows wherever it pleases. You hear its sound, but you cannot tell where it comes from or where it is going" (John 3:8). He was telling us that no one can control the Holy Spirit nor conjure up its power, but if one waits patiently, there will be an answer.

I learned about this way of having a born-again experience from reading the Catholic mystics, especially *The Spiritual Exercises of Ignatius of Loyola*. Ignatius, a founder of the Jesuit order, was once a soldier, and it was only when he spent a long time in a hospital bed recovering from a battle wound that his heart and mind focused on God. Like most Catholic mystics, he developed an intense desire to experience a "oneness" with God. Gradually, he came to feel an intense yearning for the kind of spiritual purity that he believed would enable him to experience the fullness of God's presence within. This drove Ignatius to explore ways of praying and studying the Bible that would provide this blessing. *The Spiritual*

Exercises has become a rich resource for Christians of all denominational persuasions who seek a deep intimacy with God.

After the Reformation, we Protestants left behind much that was troubling about the Roman Catholicism of the fifteenth century. I am convinced that we left too much behind. The methods of praying employed by the likes of Ignatius have become precious to me. With the help of some Catholic saints, my prayer life has deepened. Ignatius and other Catholic mystics such as Teresa of Avila have been of incredible help to me in developing a kind of praying in which God becomes a real and felt presence.

It's hard to describe just what happens in this centering prayer. No words are spoken, and none are heard. Mother Teresa once explained to an interviewer that when she prayed, she often said nothing to God. She just listened. When asked what God said to her as she prayed, she answered, "Nothing! God Listens!" Then she added, "If you don't understand what I am talking about, I can't explain it to you." I *do* know what she was talking about. The Psalmist described it poetically by saying, "it is the deep speaking to the deep." In another place, the Bible says that such prayers are "groanings that cannot be uttered."

When I rise after engaging in this centering kind of prayer, I sense a fullness in my soul. With that fullness comes awareness that God is a living and guiding presence within me. I feel like I will be led into encounters with others in which I will have opportunities to share something of what God has given me. One rather dramatic example of this took place one day as I stood on a street corner on the campus of the University of Pennsylvania, where I once taught. As I was waiting for the traffic light to change, I heard the Duck Lady come up behind me. We called this homeless woman the Duck Lady because she made an incessant quacking sound wherever she went. She seemed to be omnipresent on campus, so it was no surprise when I heard her. "Quack! Quack! Quack!" There she was, standing beside me.

Then something that verged on the supernatural happened. I turned to her, and she turned to me. Our eyes met and we *connected*. With all the spiritual energy that had flowed into me during my morning prayers, I focused on her. I didn't just look *at* her. I looked *into* her. I somehow felt empowered to reach down into the depths of her being, and I had an eerie sensation that I had touched her soul. What surprised me even more was that she was doing the same thing to me. I could feel her spiritually pouring herself into me.

She stopped her quacking. I had never heard of her doing that—but in that moment, she stopped. Then she lifted her eyes and looked around at the sky and the trees and the people nearby, and she said, "It's wonderful! It really is wonderful, isn't it? It's really wonderful!"

Before I could answer, the traffic light changed, and several people rushed by us. As one of them brushed past the Duck Lady, I watched her head jerk ever so slightly. Then she fell back into her schizophrenic state. As she wandered across the street and disappeared into a crowd, I once again heard the quacking sound. Standing motionless on that street corner, I wondered to myself what might have happened if I could have held on to her just a little longer—perhaps just a minute or two more. Then, maybe, the deliverance would not have been temporary. Just maybe, something more might have happened.

Maybe you're thinking, "He's a sociologist. Doesn't he realize that what she really needs is a psychotherapist or a psychiatrist?" The answer is "Yes!" But when the psychotherapists and psychiatrists have done all that they can to no avail, I believe that there is still "a balm in Gilead" that can heal the troubled soul. That balm becomes available to me when, in prayer, the Holy Spirit saturates my soul. In centering prayer, something happens to me that is strange and blessed. I feel the Spirit expanding within me "like a fountain of living water," as Jesus said, and I begin to experience a transforming presence and a sense of empowerment from God.

The second essential discipline that I believe will give depth to your spirituality is what is called "contemplative Bible reading."

There are many different ways to read the Bible. It can be read as a theological textbook from which doctrine can be extracted. It can be read as a history book that provides a glimpse into what went on in the lives of the strange and wonderful characters who created Israel and, later, the church. It even can be read as literature, marked by poetry and brilliant narratives. (In fact, it's often studied this way in university classes.) But in contemplative Bible reading, Scripture is read like a love letter.

Should you get a love letter, you'll read that letter over and over again. The literal meaning of the words will become secondary to what you read between the lines under the influence of your imagination. It will be as though the person you love is right there with you; you will feel a loving presence and an indescribable connectedness with that person. Each time you read it, you will likely find new meaning and feel new emotions. That is the way it is with contemplative Bible reading. Needless to say, you can't read the Bible that way unless you are already in love with Jesus. That's why I told you to start with centering prayer, because in centering prayer, you fall ever deeper in love with Jesus and you increasingly feel Jesus loving you back. The presence of his love within is what prepares you for contemplative Bible reading. Without his Spirit, the Bible is just a fascinating book; but with his Spirit vibrating within your soul, it can become a living love letter addressed especially to you.

Some people are committed to reading the Bible from beginning to end and cover to cover. I have a friend who proudly tells me that he does that every year because he wants to reacquaint himself with its contents. I have never read the Bible that way. To be honest, I don't think I could. Those genealogies in the Bible get me down. There's a place for scholarly Bible study and even for reading the Bible from cover to cover. It's important to know the contents of the Scriptures. But it is even more important to let the Spirit speak to you through Scripture and mystically teach your heart what reason alone can never know.

I'm quite selective in what I read. Every day, I read a few verses from one of the Gospels, and then I meditate on what I have read, letting God's Spirit teach me things in the sacred moments that follow. Sometimes I'll read the same few verses over and over, waiting for the Holy Spirit to make the words into sacramental food to feed my hungry soul.

Sometimes in the evening I pray one of the Psalms. That's right! I said *pray* the Psalms! That's another way of doing contemplative Bible reading. I learned that from some monks in the Benedictine order. They showed me that the Psalms can give expression to almost every emotion arising in the human heart and mind. The Psalms enable me to externalize my feelings—and sometimes they are ugly feelings. When I give voice to them as I pray the Psalms, God can deal with them and heal my sin-sick soul.

I don't confine myself to the Gospels and the Psalms. At least once a week, I spend time contemplatively reading from the Epistles. Also, I make sure to give some attention every week to passages in the Hebrew Scriptures such as the powerful writings of the Prophets. But I have to admit that when all is said and done, it's the Gospels that do the most for me. The Gospels help me to get a sense of what it must have been like to walk and talk with Jesus back there in ancient Israel. After reading the Gospels, I read the rest of the Bible through a grid created by Jesus's teachings. I understand whatever else I read in the Scriptures through its relationship to him.

Whatever you do, don't rush through your Bible reading. Let the words roll around in your heart and mind. Allow time for God to say something meant especially for you—something that will bless you, lead you, inspire you, change you.

If you are going to develop spiritual depth, you must be part of a support group that will nurture you spiritually and hold you accountable as you try to live a life marked by Christian integrity. It is easy to become lax in your spiritual disciplines of prayer and Bible reading. It is easy to be lulled into a lifestyle wherein you forget to do those things that are essential to staying alive spiritually.

Don't forget that we Evangelicals believe that there are demonic forces at work in the world that seek to hinder your growth into Christian maturity. A support group provides a strong countervailing influence against those forces and tendencies by regularly checking up on you. I believe that being part of a support group is absolutely essential. In fact, if you don't have an accountability group, I don't think you have much of a chance over the long haul of living a consistent Christian life.

"Wherever two or three are gathered together in my name, there am I in the midst of them," Jesus said (Matthew 18:20). I take Jesus at his word. I believe that something mystical can happen in the context of a support group. As members of a support group interact with one another—sharing what is going on in their lives, talking about their respective spiritual experiences, praying together, deepening their friendship, and asking probing questions of one another—a special awareness of Christ's presence can emerge.

While it is always fun to be with the three other men in my support group, sometimes we receive a kind of special blessing from our little gatherings. Meeting in the back room of Joe's Place, a little coffee shop in Wayne, Pennsylvania (our own version of Cheers), we make a lot of noise as we joke with one another, but there are times when our voices become hushed and our conversations are pervaded by deep feelings and spiritual inklings. I am reluctant to use the word *blessing* for what we experience at such times because I have an aversion to the kind of "God talk" that people sometimes use to show off their religiosity. But I don't know any other word to describe what God gives to us at such times. On some occasions when I've been troubled, what I experience with my friends has helped me to find peace. My support group has lifted me up emotionally from depression, and has encouraged me to be confident in the face of difficult challenges. This small circle of friends has given me wise counsel when I've needed to make my way through complex situations.

Decisionmaking can be very difficult for me, especially when the decision might shape my life's course. Often, I become very confused over whether a given decision is God's will or nothing more than an egoistic desire. That is when my support group can be of enormous help.

One time, a Christian college considered me for its presidency. My friends didn't say much as the search committee gave me serious consideration. I suppose that they assumed that the search committee soon would realize that I just wasn't cut out for such a job. But when I made the final cut, the friends in my support group decided that it was time to act. They sat me down and let me know that a college presidency just wasn't for me. They pointed out that my personality and style caused me to shoot from the hip on controversial issues, and that a college president could not do that sort of thing. They let me know that if I took on the presidency of that college, I'd have to change—and then I wouldn't be me anymore—or, if I continued to operate in my usual style, I'd end up destroying the college. I capitulated to their judgment and turned down the opportunity. I thank God that my friends saved me from what could have been a disaster. In retrospect, I realize that I was being seduced by the promise of prestige rather than considering how God could best use me.

My support group also has served to check up on me, to make sure I'm living a consistent Christian life. Once, when I was out in California, I got a telephone call in my motel room at 5:00 a.m. The voice at the other end of the line asked, "Are you alone?"

I answered, "It's five in the morning, of course I'm alone."

"Just checking," my friend answered. He hung up.

If you're thinking, "How horrible that you need to be checked up on from time to time," I ask you to consider the possibility that Jimmy Swaggart and Jim Bakker might not have gotten so messed up if some good brothers in Christ had been holding them accountable.

Forming a support group isn't always easy. You'll probably need to take the initiative to get things started. You'll have to ask a good friend if he or she has considered forming such an intimate support group. You may well be surprised to hear that this person has long hungered for such a support group. In our alienated world, many people crave the intimacy a support group can provide.

Make sure that you really like any person you ask to join your support group. Only invite a person you'd enjoy dining or traveling with. Also, your support group must be made up of people who are of the same sex—

don't forget that you will be sharing the most the intimate details of your lives with one another.

Don't devote the time you spend together to Bible study. You can do that on your own. It's good to share with one another what your individual sessions of Bible study and prayer are teaching you and how they are changing you, but if you make your support group all about Bible study, I assure you that your get-togethers will soon become more of a burden than a joy. When you're with these special friends, you should be making sure that each of you is keeping up daily disciplines of Bible study and prayer, rather than making these gatherings the times to get into these spiritual exercises.

Jesus had a support group. You can name them, can't you? They were Peter, James, and John. Whenever Jesus was about to enter into some unusual spiritual experience or ordeal—for instance, his encounter with Elijah and Moses on the Mount of Transfiguration—he wanted his support group with him. The presence of these special friends was a source of encouragement and strength for him. That can help us understand why he was so sad in the Garden of Gethsemane when, in the face of the horrendous trial that lay before him on Calvary, they fell asleep. You can imagine the pathos in his voice as he woke them and asked, "Could you not tarry with me for one hour?" It's as if he were saying, "Guys, just when I needed your emotional and spiritual support the most, you fell asleep on me!" If Jesus reached out for strength and encouragement from his support group, how could any of us think we can live the life and endure the ordeals we face without a support group of our own?

I have not offered these suggestions about prayer, Bible reading, and support groups because I think they are merely good ways of staying faithful in your commitment to Christ. They are absolutely essential. Without them, you will not be able to grow spiritually into the kind of people God wants you to be. It will be only a matter of time before you drift into spiritual deadness and conformity with the many destructive values that permeate the dominant culture. In Scripture we are told, "Be not conformed to the world." These guidelines are essential to preserving your integrity as Christians.

Sincerely,
Tony

4

■ Why We Witness

Dear Timothy and Junia,

In my last letter, I wrote to you about three of the essential means by which you will develop into mature Christians. I left out a fourth, vitally important element of this quest: witnessing. You might think it odd that I believe that sharing your faith with others is such an important part of spiritual growth, but it really is. We are highly influenced by what we do, and you will find that telling others about the role Christ plays in your life will have a profound effect on you. The more you witness for Christ to others, the greater will be your sense of certainty about what you yourself believe. The more you witness, the more you will feel Christ alive in you and working through you.

Witnessing is at the core of Evangelicalism. Evangelicals regard winning souls to Christ as a moral obligation of the highest order. It is our Great Commission—Jesus's command to "go into all the world and preach the gospel to every creature" (Mark 16:15). There's no way you can understand how Evangelicalism grew to be so big and powerful without realizing the vital role that the winning of converts plays in our lives.

Evangelicals believe that there will be a day when each of us must stand before God to account for our lives. On that day, we will have to answer not only for the evil we've done, but also for the good we've failed to do. Listed among the latter will be the failure to share the Gospel with those who are not committed to Christ. You are required by Christ himself to share your faith. Remember that Jesus said, "Whosoever shall confess me before men, him shall the Son of Man also confess before the angels of God" (Luke 12:8).

The stakes could not be higher. Martin Niemöller, a Lutheran pastor and head of the German Confessing Church movement, which opposed Nazism during World War II, told of a recurring nightmare wherein he saw Hitler standing before the judgment seat of God. In this nightmare, Jesus came off his throne, stood alongside Hitler, and put his arm around Hitler's shoulders. Then, with pain and sorrow in his voice, Jesus asked, "Adolf! How could you have done the incredibly cruel and evil things you did?" In the dream, Adolf Hitler answered, "Because no one ever told me about your love for me and what you did for me."

Niemöller said, "At that point, I would wake up in a cold sweat and remember that, in all the meetings I had with Hitler, I could not remember once having said anything like 'My Führer! Do you know how much Jesus loves you? And that he gave himself in a crucifixion to save you? Do you realize that if you were the only person that ever lived in history, his love for you is so great that he would have come into the world and would have died just for you?'"

What might have happened to Adolf Hitler and to the world had Martin Niemöller carried out the Great Commission?

We dare not judge Niemöller for his failure, because all of us have failed to testify to Christ's salvation on occasions when we sensed we should do so. All of us have failed, time and time again, to obey Christ's command to explain the way of salvation to needy persons who have crossed our paths. But we need to remind ourselves every day that witnessing is required of those of us who take Jesus's commands seriously. Our missionaries do a lot of good through an array of wonderful social programs in Third World countries, but if they do not tell the Gospel story and invite people to surrender themselves to Christ, their work is essentially incomplete in the eyes of Evangelicals. Churches that do not challenge their members to fulfill their witnessing responsibilities by bringing their friends and family members into transforming personal relationships with Christ may teach what Evangelicals believe but fall short of doing and being what Evangelical churches are expected to do and be.

Given how Evangelicals feel about the need to get the Gospel out to the lost, you can understand why we are so driven to share the Gospel. This drive explains much about what we do and why we do it. In order to tell our story, we hold citywide crusades that bring together tens of thousands of hearers with the hope of winning the "unsaved" to Christ. We send missionaries around the world to tell the salvation story to those who have never heard it. Our people have started more than 1,500 radio stations across the United States and around the world to get our message out. We even reach Muslim countries through our radio programs. Communist countries such as Cuba and China are unable to keep us off their airwaves. James Dobson, who hosts the most famous Evangelical radio show, *Focus on the Family*, reaches at least a million people through daily broadcasts on more than six thousand stations worldwide.

Nowadays, we Evangelicals are using television with great effectiveness, beaming programs to almost every corner of the earth. We even have our own television networks. The programs we put on have become increasingly sophisticated. We have musical talent that rivals the best the secular world can offer. The technological expertise and equipment that some of our people bring to television broadcasting is of the highest order. Listeners and viewers send in tens of millions of dollars monthly to keep Evangelical shows on the air twenty-four hours a day.

I don't think that many people are directly won to Christ through these shows—but I know that these radio and television shows are responsible for a great deal of what is increasingly called "pre-Evangelicalsm." They provide teachings that prepare people for the kinds of decisionmaking that occurs when listeners and viewers are confronted in more directly personal ways. These programs often explain how psychological and spiritual needs can be met when people surrender their lives to Christ. When those who tune in to these religious broadcasts go to mass meetings and hear famous evangelists such as Billy Graham, TD Jakes, and Luis Palau (all of whom, incidentally, became famous through religious radio and TV shows), they are positioned to answer "yes" when invited to raise their hands and accept Christ.

We have established our own entertainment industry as well. Gospel music has become a billion-dollar industry. Every summer, hordes of young people attend outdoor concerts to hear Christian rock bands in crowds that rival Woodstock's in size. We older folks fill civic auditoriums and concert halls—even famed ones such as Radio City Music Hall—to hear the music of Bill and Gloria Gaither and a goodly number of others who have made country-gospel music a mainstay in Evangelical circles. Given the fame and financial rewards involved, I cannot be certain that all of these recording artists do what they do only to spread the Gospel. But the Gaithers, whom I know personally, are among the most committed Christians in the business. I can assure you that they see their music as a means for reaching people with the good news that God loves them and that Christ died for them.

We Evangelicals are also big in the book business. Our authors publish thousands of new titles each year. At a time when sales of secular books are declining, sales of books from Evangelical publication houses are soaring. With Christian bookstores in just about every community, we are making Evangelical books available to almost everyone in America. Not only do we publish books spelling out what we believe and how the Christian life should be lived, we're also producing novels for adults, comic books for teenagers, and a variety of books and audio tapes for children. We are inundating the country with publications promoting Evangelicalism in all of its forms and variations.

It is hard for anyone in America to escape our outreach efforts. We Evangelicals have made great strides in establishing various clubs and organizations to reach young people in the nation's high schools and colleges. Organizations such as Young Life, Youth for Christ, Campus Crusade, and InterVarsity Christian Fellowship are active on campuses everywhere. The Promise Keepers movement fills football stadiums with millions of men who are affected and changed by what they hear from Evangelical speakers. Now there are massive gatherings for women, called Women of Faith, that imitate the Promise Keeper rallies.

Behind all of this activism is the conviction held by most Evangelicals that people without Christ are lost souls who will be doomed to endless punishment in Hell when this life is over. Because we know how offensive it can seem when we say that people can be saved only through accepting Christ, we are not always entirely up front about it. When prominent Evangelical leaders such as Rick Warren of the huge Saddleback Church in Southern California and even Billy Graham are asked on television talk shows such as *Larry King Live* and the *Charlie Rose Show* whether there is any way to Heaven apart from Jesus Christ, they show great discomfort. There is almost always a poignant pause and shifting in posture before they reluctantly answer, "No, there is not."

The talk-show host is often incredulous: "You mean to tell me that good-living Jews and Muslims are lost? That people like Gandhi are doomed?"

The Evangelical leader may shift in his or her seat, trying to weasel out of appearing narrow-minded and exclusive. A typical response might be, "Of course, none of us is God, so none of us can know for sure who is saved and who is lost." But, ultimately, an Evangelical's answer has to be, "In all likelihood, yes." Any other answer would leave him or her open to severe criticism from other Evangelicals.

Over the past few years, some Evangelicals have been seeking an "out" from the exclusive claims of traditional Evangelical theology. Evangelical Universalists, whose ranks are growing, hold an unconventional understanding of the doctrine of grace. While they hold to the belief that there is no salvation apart from what Christ accomplished on the cross, these Evangelicals declare that Christ's salvation is for everyone—Christian and non-Christian alike. They believe that, in the end, everyone will be saved. They refer to such verses as Romans 5:18 to make the case that because through one man's sin (Adam's) all humanity was condemned, so by one man's sacrifice (Christ's) all humanity was declared righteous. For Universalists, *all* means all.

Universalists tell a story to drive home their point. The story is set in Heaven. Peter handles admissions at the pearly gates. Paul, acting as the administrator of the celestial kingdom, takes a monthly census of Heaven's inhabitants. Each time Paul counts the number of people in Heaven, his number far exceeds the number of admittances that Peter has registered. This discrepancy mystifies them both for quite a while. Then, one day, Paul runs up to Peter and excitedly shouts, "Peter! Peter! I figured out why our numbers don't match. I figured out why there are so many more people in Heaven than you're letting in at the pearly gates. It's Jesus! It's Jesus! He keeps sneaking people over the wall!" Jesus, they believe, offers unlimited grace—in contrast to a church that, if it had its way, would keep many people out.

"God exists whether you believe it or not! God created you whether you believe it or not! The Bible is an infallible message from God whether you believe it or not! So why can't I say that Jesus is your Savior whether you believe it or not?" This argument was once put to me by a young Evangelical Universalist. I answered him by saying that the Bible makes it clear that one cannot be saved without believing in Jesus, repenting of sin, and surrendering to transformation by the Spirit. "Of course!" he replied. He went on to say that, sooner or later, everyone *will* accept Christ—those who reject him in this life will have a chance to surrender to him in the hereafter. "Jesus never gives up on anybody," he argued. "Isn't that what it says in the eighth chapter of Romans, where we read that not even death can separate us from God?" he asked. Then he quoted from 1 Peter 3:18–19, offering this passage as biblical evidence that Jesus (whom he called "the hound of Heaven") continues to pursue the unsaved even after their lives have ended and to plead with them until, in the words of Scripture, "at the name of Jesus, every knee shall bow and every tongue confess that Jesus Christ is Lord." Eventually, he concluded, everyone gets saved.

When I told this young man that talk like that put him outside of the Evangelical fold, he responded, "So what! Evangelicalism is too narrow for me anyway." He explained that he is part of a new movement known as "the emergent church," which holds to many Evangelical beliefs but is not as "narrow-minded" as he considers many mainstream Evangelicals to be. He added, "I still consider myself an Evangelical—even if you don't. I just don't buy into the eternal-damnation stuff that you preach."

Afterward, I did some hard thinking about what this young rebel had said. His comments made me question to what extent we traditional Evangelicals believe our own rhetoric. We certainly do not live our everyday lives as though we do. It is so easy for those of us in the Evangelical community to talk about other people's going to Hell. But if, in the depths of our being, we really believe that all who do not accept Christ are eternally lost, we should constantly be witnessing—because the thought of anyone's going to Hell without having heard about Christ should be an intolerable burden to bear. When asked what I really believe, I'm a bit shaky. I believe what Evangelicals traditionally have believed, but I somehow feel, on a gut level, that God's grace reaches beyond the narrow confines of my theology. I have extreme difficulty accepting that those who have never had a chance even to hear about Jesus—for instance, those who live in remote places such as Nepal or in isolated tribes in the

Amazon—are doomed by a just God to eternal damnation. I know that, even here in America, some people grow up in such adverse settings that coming to know about God's love as expressed in Christ is near impossible. In spite of what Evangelical theology prescribes, I struggle with the belief that their fate is eternal separation from God.

I'm not the only one who is burdened with such questions. The apostle Paul raises the same questions in Romans 2:13–16 as he considers the fate of those who live up to the best that their consciences direct them to do but never come to grips with biblical truths.

Then there's the question of people who *may* know Jesus personally but do not know him by that name. While visiting a Buddhist monastery in China, a friend of mine noticed a monk seated peacefully in deep meditation. My friend felt a strong impulse to disturb the monk and share the Gospel with him. As my friend explained the story of Christ's sacrificial gift of salvation, he noticed that the monk was visibly moved. Then my friend asked the monk the simple question, "Will you surrender to Christ and invite him to be a living presence within you?"

The monk answered with dismay, "Invite him into my life? How can I accept him when he is already within me? I have known him for many years, but I did not know his name. Even as you were telling me about what he did for me, his spirit was prompting me from within to affirm what you told me. Thank you for giving his presence within me a name."

My friend was left with some disturbing questions. Did that monk have a saving relationship with Christ before he ever heard the Gospel story? How essential is it to know the name of Jesus? If experiencing Jesus without knowing him by name is enough, then how are we to take the verse, "for there is none other name under heaven given among men, whereby we must be saved" (Acts 4:12)?

I once heard a story from a young English evangelist. He told me about the day Charlie Peace, a well-known criminal in London, was hanged—February 25, 1879. The Anglican Church, which had a ceremony for nearly everything, even had a ceremony for hangings. So, when Charlie Peace was marched to the gallows, a priest walked behind him and read these words from a prayer book: "Those who die without Christ experience Hell, which is the pain of forever dying without the release which death itself can bring."

When these chilling words were read, Charlie Peace stopped in his tracks, turned to the priest, and shouted in his face, "Do you believe that? Do you believe that?"

The priest, taken aback by this sudden verbal assault, stammered for a moment and then said, "Well . . . I . . . suppose I do."

"Well, I don't," said Charlie. "But if I did, I'd get down on my hands and knees and crawl all over Great Britain, even if it were paved with pieces of broken glass, if I could just rescue one person from what you just told me."

If we Evangelicals *really* believe what we say about the eternal damnation of unsaved souls, how can we sleep at night? What would it mean to live every minute of every day *really* believing that our family members and friends could die at any moment and be doomed to eternal punishment for their sins because they have not accepted Christ? But imagine the consequences of giving up our belief that those who die without Christ are eternally lost. It is, after all, that belief that is usually viewed as essential for our zealous drive to evangelize that has made modern-day Evangelicalism the most dynamic Christian movement since the New Testament days.

Sincerely,
Tony

5

■ How We Witness

Dear Junia and Timothy,

As I explained in my last letter, witnessing is essential to Evangelicalism. It is one of the things that most distinguishes us from believers in mainline denominational churches. Whereas they believe most of the same things we Evangelicals do, few mainline church members demonstrate a passion for sharing their faith commitments with others. Most mainline denominational Christians seem willing to live and let live when it comes to religion, and consider it impolite to talk about religion at social gatherings. Sometimes they even seem embarrassed by the prospect of having to tell non-Christians about what they believe.

We Evangelicals, on the other hand, are always looking for opportunities to tell others about who Christ is, what he's done for us, and what he can do for them. Sometimes our zeal to share our faith can make us obnoxious or, if it drives people away from religion, even counterproductive.

When I was a teenager, there was a woman in our neighborhood who seemed oblivious of how people reacted to her witnessing. You couldn't talk to her about anything without being reminded that you were a sinner in need of salvation. If you said, "Good morning. How are you?" she would say something like, "Wonderful, because I have Jesus in my heart—and you could have the same kind of joy in your heart if you would just accept Jesus as your personal savior." When people saw her coming, they would run the other way.

This kind of aggressive witnessing remains a problem because it is generally offensive and often prevents people from ever giving the Gospel story a fair hearing. Søren Kierkegaard, the Danish existentialist, once said there are those who tell lies in such a way that you think they are telling you the truth. He went on to suggest that far more dangerous are those who tell the truth in such a way that you think they are telling you a lie. When the Gospel is presented with little regard for the sensitivities of others, it may readily be rejected not because of its content but because of *how* it has been delivered.

During my ten years on the faculty of an Ivy League university, there was a vocal Christian organization on campus that managed to alienate most of the secular students. They would, for instance, write letters to the school newspaper condemning the school's Gay and Lesbian Task Force, declaring that gay and lesbian people were an abomination to God and doomed to Hell unless they let Jesus change them into heterosexuals. Such letters usually had a P.S. that read, "By the way, God really loves you." It would be hard to convince anyone who read such hateful letters that those who wrote them were trying to witness about a loving God who seeks intimacy with all people, and especially with those whom society treats as outcasts.

I think that the manner in which some Evangelicals witness for Christ can make the good news about God's sacrificial love into something others find unbelievable. To use biblical phraseology, such witnessing "makes the Word of God of none effect" (Mark 7:13). We are required by Jesus himself to be bold witnesses of his teachings and the salvation story. But we must be careful not to turn people away from Christ by our style of witnessing.

The other extreme is just as bad, if not worse. Too often, I hear Christians in mainline denominations saying things like, "I don't have to talk about my faith. I live it! My witness is the life I live before others, and I believe I so live out what it means to be a Christian that words are not really necessary."

What arrogance! Do any of us live out our faith so compellingly that anyone merely observing us will be swept into giving himself or herself over to God? Of course not! The only people who seem truly righteous are people we don't know very well. All of us have flaws that could easily disillusion anyone who turns to us for guidance on how to live a Christian life. I always tell people, "Don't look at me too closely; you'll be disappointed. But if you look to Christ, you will find what you're looking for."

I believe that there is something mystical at the heart of effective witnessing. That is why all witnessing should be preconditioned by prayer. Your efforts to win others to Christ can be greatly enhanced if, each day, you prepare yourself for witnessing by setting aside time to surrender to an infilling of God's Spirit. Witnessing requires spiritual energy, and that is one reason I so emphasized centering prayer in my last letter to you. When you surrender to the Holy Spirit in the quietude of prayer, you will recognize what the prophet Isaiah was talking about when he wrote, "They that wait upon the Lord shall renew their strength" (Isaiah 40:31). The spiritual energy derived from such praying will provide a unique capacity to spiritually connect with people— and that is a requisite for effectively sharing your faith with others.

The apostle Paul once reminded those whose lives had been changed through his witnessing that he did not come to them "with excellency of words," but in the power of the Holy Spirit (I Cor. 2:1–5). The Spirit not only must be in you, empowering and guiding your words, but also must be encompassing and readying the other person. When the Spirit has done the preparing, you will have just the right words to say; you will even be

aware of just the right moment to speak. There is something mystical about witnessing, and timing is of incredible importance.

Personally, when I am witnessing, I usually tell the
person my intentions. On some occasions, I have invited
someone to breakfast or lunch, explaining ahead of time
that I want to spend a little time talking about my faith
commitments. I'm not sure this will work for you, but it
works quite well for me. I find that people tend to appreciate my straightforwardness.

The hellfire-and-brimstone approach makes me
more than a bit uncomfortable, and it is often counterproductive. Some people would condemn me for not
preaching God's condemnation on all who refuse to believe the Gospel and surrender themselves to Christ. But
I think that starting off by telling people that they are
lost sinners in danger of eternal punishment seems contrary to the tone of the Bible. Jesus said that he did not
come into the world to condemn the world, but that the
world through him might be saved (John 3:17). Instead
of focusing on God's judgment, I start by explaining that
I believe that God has a specific and significant purpose
for every person, and that our surrendering to Christ is
the beginning of our living out that purpose.

Many people wonder if there is any meaning to their
lives. I believe that God sent Christ to initiate a movement through which *the world that is* could be transformed into *the world that ought to be*. And so I tell people

that becoming a Christian means deciding to participate in that movement, to live out the unique role God has especially prescribed for you. For many, it comes as a wonderful revelation to learn that God has given every one of us a purpose, and that coming to Christ is the means by which each individual can embrace his or her unique purpose. It's a good idea to have a Bible available when you witness so that you can show your friend verses that back up this assertion—for example, Ephesians 2:10: "For we are his workmanship, created in Christ Jesus unto good works, which God hath before ordained that we should walk in them."

When Jesus was here on earth, he preached that the kingdom of God was at hand. That kingdom will be very different from our own world, according to Isaiah 65:17–25. In our world, the elderly are often neglected, and 35,000 children die each day as a result of starvation and malnutrition-related diseases. But in the kingdom that God wants to create here on earth, infants will be cared for, and elderly people will live out their lives in good health (v. 20). Parents, in this kingdom, will not worry that their children will be destroyed because of such tragedies as gang warfare, drugs, or unwanted pregnancies (v. 23). This re-created society willed by God will be one of justice and environmental responsibility, where people plant vineyards and eat safely of the fruit (v. 22), and neither hurt nor destroy one another (v. 25). Each and every one of us is invited to join God in creating this kingdom on earth. By living out the specific roles that God has planned for each of us, we imbue our lives with meaning. I believe that the invitation to live out such a destiny can provide a crucial incentive for persons to become Christians.

I've described my approach to witnessing, which involves explaining how surrendering to Christ can satisfy a person's quest for meaning. But you should know that there are a host of other reasons why people become receptive to the Gospel story. You should choose your approach to sharing the Gospel story in light of the circumstances of those to whom you are speaking.

Sometimes people turn to Christ in response to serious troubles in their lives. In crisis, people often become aware that human ingenuity and effort are sometimes inadequate. At such times of crisis people often have a heightened awareness that they need God's help.

It was in a time of crisis that Chuck Colson, a White House adviser during the Nixon administration, became born again. Colson was a high-flying young lawyer, and it must have been a heady time when he found himself in the Oval Office advising the president of the United States on legal matters. But when the Watergate scandal erupted, Colson found himself involved in the disastrous cover-up. When his lies became public knowledge, he found himself not only disgraced but behind bars.

A good friend of mine, Doug Coe, is the head of an organization called The Fellowship. The Fellowship, perhaps most famous for sponsoring the National Prayer Breakfast, is an informal network of Christians who make a special effort to witness to powerful people in business and government who are seldom reached by the church. As the founder and leader of The Fellowship, Coe made it his special concern to regularly visit the imprisoned Colson. These visits resulted in a friendship between the two men. Eventually, Coe was able to convince Colson that God had a significant and good future in store for him if he would turn his life over to Christ. Out of his despair, Colson made his decision to be born again.

Colson was traumatized by prison, and upon his release he sought to help others who find themselves behind bars. He founded Prison Fellowship, a worldwide organization that ministers to those who are incarcerated. Through Prison Fellowship, tens of thousands of inmates have been brought into transforming relationships with Christ and have found the kind of hope Colson himself found when he became a born-again Christian.

Difficult or tragic circumstances—a diagnosis of cancer, the arrest of a teenage son, the collapse of a marriage—can make a person acutely aware of the need for God's help. But I'd urge you to be especially careful in choosing how you share Christ with people in such situations. Forthright witnessing at such times can anger people who are hurting, and they may justifiably accuse you of exploiting their emotional vulnerability. Your first obligation is to become a friend to troubled persons. This takes time. You must pray to God to create in you a love for those who suffer. Only when a suffering person is confident of your love can you dare to call him or her to commit to Christ. Before you carry out the Great Commission, you ought to live out the Great Commandment: "Thou shalt love the Lord thy God with all thy heart, and with all thy soul, and with all thy mind, and with all thy strength. This is the first commandment. And the second is like it, namely this: Thou shalt love thy neighbor as thyself" (Mark 12:30–31).

Finally, some will reach out for Christ in the face of the ultimate tragedy, which is death. As death draws near, fear can be overwhelming. The dying almost always yearn for some good news affirming that this life is not all there is. Once, a dear family friend named Helen became painfully aware that her life was coming to an end. Helen was an interesting elderly woman who had led a colorful life as a traveling salesperson. During the final years of Helen's life, my wife, Peggy, had befriended her. Peggy visited Helen often, took her shopping, accompanied her to the doctor, and looked after her in a variety of other ways.

On several occasions, I tried to approach Helen with the salvation story, but each time she blew me off. Then Helen had a serious fall and broke her hip. Her condition went from bad to worse, and it was soon evident that she was going to die. Helen changed as she lay on a hospital bed knowing that her end was near. This once self-assured old lady was filled with fear.

On the eve of her death, Helen told Peggy that she knew she was dying, and that she was filled with anxieties. She asked Peggy if there was any help for her from God. Peggy, by her own admission, was not very much into being a Christian at that time, and she certainly would not have considered herself an Evangelical. But she is the daughter of a Baptist pastor and was raised in the church, so she knew all the right things to say to lead someone into a salvation experience.

Something extraordinary happened that evening as Peggy told Helen about Jesus and what he had accomplished for her on the cross. Not only did Helen have a faith experience that enabled her to face death courageously, but, in telling Helen about Jesus, Peggy herself came to an assurance of her own salvation. As she was witnessing to Helen, Christ became very real to Peggy. Ever since then, she has been intensely committed to ministering for Christ—especially to suffering people. This is the kind of mystical experience I referred to at the beginning of this letter. Peggy's encounter with Helen is an excellent example of how witnessing to others can have a powerful impact your own spiritual life.

In closing, there is one other thing I feel I should tell you about witnessing: Remember to ask the person to

make a decision for Christ. Don't just leave things hang-
ing. My own experiences have proved just how crucial
this part of witnessing is.

A few years ago, I was invited to a western state to
speak at the governor's annual prayer breakfast. As is
customary at these sorts of things, the governor invited
me to dinner the preceding evening. During the meal, I
asked about the previous year's speaker. The governor
responded in detail, explaining each point the speaker
had made in his talk.

It was obvious that the speaker had touched all the
bases in outlining and making clear the way of salvation.
In fact, I couldn't think of anything to add to what he
had said. I had no doubt that the governor fully understood what was involved in becoming a Christian, and
so I asked if he had ever made a decision to surrender
his life to Christ. There was a long and poignant pause.
Finally, the governor admitted that he had not. I asked
him why.

He answered, "Because nobody ever asked me to."

"Well, I'm asking right now," I responded. "Will you
say 'yes' to the invitation to surrender your life to
Christ?"

"Yes!" he answered, and then we prayed together.

In the business world they call this "closing the
deal." I am surprised by how many people who witness
are reluctant to take this essential final step. They tell
the whole story and lay out all the details as to what is

involved—but then they don't offer the invitation to give one's life to Christ. If you think that asking the question isn't important, you're wrong. Don't be embarrassed when it comes to pressing people to make decisions for Christ.

I've said a lot here about what you should and shouldn't do in witnessing. It is important to do and say the right things and avoid the pitfalls. But this is not the most critical part of witnessing. When I told you that there is something mystical in witnessing, I was getting at the essence of what enables a person to be born again. It is the Holy Spirit who converts people, not you or me. Ultimately, it is the Holy Spirit who motivates people to trust in Christ for salvation, and it is the Holy Spirit who gives power and relevance to any of our spoken words. Don't forget that!

With that in mind, I urge you to get on with it and witness as the Spirit leads you. So much depends on your willingness to be used by God. I've got more to say about that, but I'll save it for another letter.

Sincerely,
Tony

6

■ Why the Church Is Important

Dear Timothy and Junia,

Right now I want you to do some careful thinking about the role that the institutional church will play in your lives. Many young Evangelicals are a bit leery of getting too involved in the life of a local congregation. Some can tell painful stories of bad experiences with institutionalized Christianity.

In America, Evangelical churches have often been bastions of conservatism, providing support for the status quo. For example, many of our leaders were reluctant to lend their support to the civil-rights movement when their help was desperately needed. More recently, some of our leaders have allowed male chauvinism to continue unchallenged. Unfortunately, these kinds of lapses have earned Evangelical churches a reputation for being reactionary and even contrary to the teachings of Jesus Christ. When secularists are asked about Evangelical churches, they often say that they consider our churches and other Evangelical institutions to be anti-gay and sexist.

It is certainly true that our congregations have at times compromised the radical requirements of discipleship prescribed by Christ, and you may find yourself put off by the church because of its failure to be faithful to his teachings. But I would urge you to consider this carefully, and to think about the words of St. Augustine: "The church is a whore, but she's my mother." That statement brilliantly conveys how I feel about the church. It is easy for me, like so many of the young Evangelicals I know, to note the ways the church has been unfaithful as the bride of Christ. You don't have to look too hard to see that the Evangelical church in America has a great propensity for reducing Christianity to a validation of our society's middle-class way of life. Unquestionably, the church too often has socialized our young people into adopting culturally established values of success, rather than calling them into the kind of countercultural nonconformity that Scripture requires of Christ's followers (Romans 12:1–2).

Why, then, do I encourage you to participate in organized religion and commit yourself to a specific local congregation? Because, as Augustine made clear, *the church is still your mother*. It is she who taught you about Jesus. I want you to remember that the Bible teaches that Christ loves the church and gave himself for it (Ephesians 5:25). That's a preeminent reason why you dare not decide that you don't need the church. Christ's church is called his bride (II Cor. 11:2), and his love for her makes him faithful to her even when she is not faithful to him.

Through the ages, God has used the church to keep alive and pass down the story of what Christ has done for us. It is the church's witness that has kept the world aware that Christ is alive today, offering help and strength to those who trust in him. The story of Christ would have been lost during the Dark Ages if the church had not sustained it in monasteries where the Scriptures were laboriously hand-copied while barbarians were tearing down the rest of Western civilization. Church councils have protected Christianity from heresies by examining new theologies. Today, it is against two thousand years of church tradition that our modern-day interpretations of Scripture are tested. In short, it is the church that has preserved the Gospel and delivered it into our hands.

Where would most of us be without the church? Most Evangelicals have the church to thank for the Sunday-school classes that taught us what the Bible says and paved the way for our eventual decisions to commit our lives to Christ. Stop and consider the importance of the church's worship and liturgical functions. Even if we Evangelicals aren't likely to call them sacraments, as the Roman Catholics do, we still recognize the importance of certain ceremonial rituals. For instance, baptism is an important public declaration of faith that initiates new members into the fellowship of our churches. In baptism, new Christians become part of a body of fellow believers who are called to spiritually encourage one another and hold one another responsible for consistent Christian living. The extent to which churches live up to such obligations varies from congregation to congregation.

Holy Communion is another ritual of our churches that cannot be taken for granted. Even if most Evangelicals view the bread and wine as only symbolic of the body and blood of Christ—and there are many Evangelicals who view them as more than that—the role that those symbols play in our lives cannot and should not be minimized. Holy Communion focuses our faith on Christ's sacrificial death, which delivered us from our sins and signaled his conquest over the demonic forces of the universe.

My earliest memories of church services involve the sacred specialness of Communion Sundays. Before I understood any of the theological underpinnings of Communion services, I sensed that there was some kind of mysterious blessing in the air on these days. I felt an awe and reverence falling upon the congregation, and I was aware that something special, something with inklings of the supernatural, was happening. I realized early on that there was a sacred meaning to the bread and wine that demanded a hushed solemnity from everyone present.

Sitting with my parents at a Communion service when I was very young, perhaps six or seven years old, I became aware of a young woman in the pew in front of us who was sobbing and shaking. The minister had just finished reading the passage of Scripture written by Paul that says, "Whosoever shall eat the bread and drink the cup of the Lord unworthily, shall be guilty of the body and blood of the Lord" (1 Corinthians 11:27). As the Communion plate with its small pieces of bread was passed to the crying woman before me, she waved it away and then lowered her head in despair. It was then that my Sicilian father leaned over her shoulder and, in his broken English, said sternly, "Take it, girl! It was meant for you. Do you hear me?"

She raised her head and nodded—and then she took the bread and ate it. I knew that at that moment some kind of heavy burden was lifted from her heart and mind. Since then, I have always known that a church that could offer Communion to hurting people as a special gift from God.

Some claim that they can worship alone, and I do not question their claims. Indeed, those who cannot be alone with God are not fit for community. But the positive experience of worshipping alone does not contradict my argument that something different happens when Christians come together in corporate worship. The sociologist Emile Durkheim recognized that at such a gathering a unique feeling of oneness often emerges—he called it "collective effervescence." He meant that there is some kind of shared emotion and psychic power that can be experienced only in communal worship. It doesn't always happen, but when it does, those who share in this ecstasy keep coming back for more.

I belong to an African American church, and on those special days when the congregation "really gets down, and the Spirit breaks loose," as my pastor says—those are days when that collective effervescence is especially evident—people say afterward, "Oh, we had church today, didn't we?" For them, on those days the church becomes something more than a gathering of people in a sanctuary. It becomes a happening. But such happenings would never happen if there weren't "an earthen vessel," as Paul called it, to contain them. That's what the church is. In spite of all of its flaws and shortcomings, it is the "earthen vessel" that can serve as a home for sacred happenings and the special fellowship that the Greek New Testament calls *koinonia*.

At Eastern University, where I teach sociology, we have weekly chapel services. Attendance is voluntary, but students have been showing up in such large numbers over the past few years that we have had to move our weekly worship services from the school chapel to the gym. It's not the speakers that draw the crowds, but the worship. These worship services feature "praise music." As an old guy, I have difficulties with this new praise/worship music, but the students love it. I see them with their hands lifted up and tears running down their cheeks as they sing love songs to God, and I realize that they are experiencing God in a way that transports them from the gym bleachers into a mystical community of holiness. I become aware of that collective effervescence wherein God's presence becomes uniquely real. There and then, I am grateful for the corporate worship that makes such things possible.

There is another reason that the church should play an important role in your lives: the church is Christ's primary instrument for bringing about social change and transforming the institutions of society to conform with his will. It is through the church that Christ has chosen to bring all principalities and powers into submission to himself (Ephesians 1:21–22).

When the apostle Paul used the phrase *principalities and powers*, he was referring to all of the suprahuman forces that influence what we think and do. Some Christians limit the meaning of these words and think that Paul was referring only to evil spirits (i.e., demons). Undoubtedly, that is part of what Paul meant. Evangelicals, especially in this postmodern age, are ready to affirm that there are demonic forces fostering havoc and evil in the world. It should be noted, however, that modern scholars such as Walter Wink and John Howard Yoder have pointed out the phrase's broader meaning. Principalities and powers, say many Biblical scholars, also include such social constructions as television, government, economic systems, and the arts. These and all other social institutions, they argue, should be understood as superhuman forces that influence human behavior. What Paul tells us in Ephesians 6:12 is that we members of the church are supposed to wrestle with these principalities and powers so that they might be transformed into institutions that enact God's will.

Allow me to give you some examples of how ordinary Christians are doing extraordinary things as they work to bring the principalities and powers under the lordship of Christ through the church. Christians in England, working together across denominational lines, have seriously influenced international policies regarding Third World debts. When the heads of the G8 nations held a summit in the city of Birmingham in 1998, Christians mobilized tens of thousands of church members to hold a prayer vigil in front of the convention hall where the meetings were held. Clare Short, who was then Britain's secretary of State for international development, told me that it was that church-sponsored prayer vigil that moved the world leaders to make the first efforts toward debt cancellation.

The collapse of apartheid in South Africa offers another dramatic example of the church's bringing principalities and powers into submission to God's will. Archbishop Tutu, the leader of the Anglican church in that country, was able to make the church into a force for justice. There can be no question as to the crucial role the church played in challenging the racism that had made black Africans into less than second-class citizens.

As young people rebelled against the oppression of the South African police, they found in Tutu a spokesperson and leader for their movement. American author (and my friend) Jim Wallis describes how, on one occasion, Tutu met with thousands of freedom-seeking young people in the cathedral of Cape Town. The atmosphere was electric with anticipation as Tutu took his place in the pulpit. He pointed to the policemen who had positioned themselves along the walls of the cathedral to intimidate the crowd. Then he lovingly spoke to the police: "Come join us! You know we will win, so why not be part of the victory?" Then he led the thousands of young people in singing freedom songs. The congregation rose to its feet, swayed to the music, and started dancing in the aisles. There was no containing these young people, who were celebrating the coming end of apartheid. The dancing spilled onto the streets, and passersby joined in. Thus, a revolution was fueled by a church that was willing to challenge oppressive principalities and powers that had once seemed unshakable.

In addition to such direct campaigns for social change, there are a host of other ways in which the church has been a powerful force for positive societal transformation. Consider what has been accomplished because of missionary work in developing nations.

Schools created by missionaries have educated most of the significant leaders in Africa, Latin America, and Asia. The professional elites in developing countries—the doctors, lawyers, engineers, and entrepreneurs—almost all owe their training to church-sponsored education. Kofi Annan is one example. In Latin America, even Marxists have to give credit to church schools for training their leaders. Fidel Castro readily testifies that his revolutionary ideas came from his childhood training in Jesuit schools. And I haven't even mentioned all the incredible work missionaries have done in the fields of medical care and agriculture in developing countries.

Some people mock the missionary efforts of the church, and claim that they have been destructive of indigenous cultures. There is some truth in what these critics say; missionaries have often made the mistake of imposing Western values and lifestyles on native peoples. But today's missionaries are much more cross-culturally sensitive than were their predecessors, and they are often trained in cultural anthropology so that they can contextualize the Gospel in ways that both employ and preserve the best of native cultures.

While I think that cultural sensitivity is essential, I don't believe that every cultural practice should be tolerated simply because it is indigenous. For instance, certain cultures allow the ceremonial sacrificing of children, and others call for the circumcision of girls upon entering puberty. I believe unequivocally that such practices should be eliminated, and I think you will, too. Likewise, I have no qualms when it comes to challenging the treatment of women in Islamic countries governed by sharia law or what remains of the caste system in India. If the work of missionaries undermines cultural patterns that are cruel and dehumanizing, I'm all for it. The sooner, the better.

There is little doubt that the tentacles of Western technology, and the social changes that come with it, sooner or later will reach out and affect every tribe and nation on earth. Given that expectation, I would prefer that preliterate societies first encounter the West via missionaries, who have the best interests and salvation of indigenous people at heart, rather than via commercial forces whose only concern is the maximizing of profits.

There is one scary thing about our desire to change the world into a societal system that is ever more like the kingdom of God. This is the triumphalist tendency, increasingly evident among us Evangelicals, to use political power to impose our will on the rest of the nation and even the rest of the world. I see this happening especially among Evangelicals identified with the Religious Right who exercise their significant influence to try to force their agenda on others. There is incredible danger in this. I hope you can understand that Evangelicals' God-ordained identity as a servant people is compromised when we adopt coercion as our means for bringing others into compliance with God's will.

Young people often tell me that they are wary of the institutional church because they believe it is filled with hypocrites. Well, it is. What these people fail to understand, however, is that it is *because* the church is filled with hypocrites that they'll be right at home in it. If they don't think their own lives are filled with hypocrisies, then they are blind to the truth. We in the church make no bones about it. We acknowledge our hypocrisy. We believe that everyone is a hypocrite, if by "hypocrite" we mean someone who does not live up to his or her declared ideals and does not practice what he or she preaches. Most of us in the church recognize that we fall short of our goals, but we acknowledge our shortcomings and have come together to help one another overcome our failures. As the old saying goes, "We're not what we ought to be, but then we're not what we used to be." The apostle Paul spoke for all of us in Philippians 3:13–14 when he acknowledged that he wasn't perfect, but was still striving to become what God wanted him to be. I guess what I'm trying to tell you is the same thing I'd tell anyone else: if you ever find the perfect church, don't join it—because your joining will ruin it!

In spite of all its flaws and shortcomings, I still believe that the church is filled, for the most part, with decent and caring people who will be there when you need them. The loving fellowship that the church often provides is exemplified in a story that a Presbyterian pastor once told me about his early days of ministry at a small country church. One day, a young woman came to the church to present her child for baptism. She had given birth to the child out of wedlock; in a small rural community, a woman who has done this can easily find herself shunned. The day of the baptism, the woman stood alone before the congregation, holding her child in her arms. The pastor hadn't recognized the awkwardness of the situation until he asked, as is customary in a baptismal service, "Who stands with this child to assure the commitments and promises herewith made will be carried out? Who will be there for this child in times of need and assure that this child is brought up in the nurture and admonition of the Lord?" At that moment, he realized that there was no godmother or godfather on hand to answer the question. But, as though on cue, the entire congregation stood and with one voice said, "We will!"

Those who think that church people are all bad should have been around on that Sunday, when they would have had a chance to see the church at its best. They would have seen the church as a nurturing community.

That kind of church is worth your time.

Sincerely,
Tony

7

▦ Getting High on Jesus

Dear Junia and Timothy,

To outsiders, we Evangelicals might seem to be part of some monolithic movement with a singular mind-set and a unified, politically conservative agenda. In reality, we are part of a family whose members have some sharp differences of opinion and worship practices that often set us at odds with one another. One of the most pronounced fissures in today's Evangelical world is the one between Pentecostal Christians and Fundamentalists.

I'm sure you've heard about Pentecostalism. It's hard to avoid it these days. Mass gatherings in arenas and stadiums across the country have drawn hundreds of thousands of followers and curious seekers. Many who are sick and physically disabled come to these gatherings hoping to find out whether Pentecostal faith healers, who figure prominently as leaders of this movement, can deliver cures from God. In this postmodern era, more and more Christians are unsatisfied with the rationalistic theologies offered by the rest of Christendom. They come to Pentecostalism with a craving for a mystical spirituality that offers emotional assurances that God is real, and they are finding what they need. Some of Pentecostalism's most prominent preachers, such as Benny Hinn, have attracted widespread attention through their regular appearances on such television shows as *Larry King Live* and major stories in *Newsweek* and *Time* magazines.

The growth of the Pentecostal wing of Evangelicalism has been phenomenal. In 1977, there were 50 million Pentecostals; ten years later, there were 200 million; and today, there are 600 million.

Pentecostalism has swept through Latin America, Africa, and a significant part of Asia. In Europe, it is generating new spiritual vitality among people who had considered themselves to be living in a post-Christian era. Here in the United States, Pentecostalism is by far the fastest-growing form of Christianity, and new Pentecostal mega-churches are springing up from coast to coast. If you doubt Pentecostalism's growing dynamism, just check out the parking lot of that new Pentecostal church in your neighborhood on Sundays.

Pentecostalism has brought a dynamism and excitement to twenty-first-century Christianity that is invigorating all kinds of churches outside of the Pentecostal sphere. It is so influential that many observers predict that it may be the only form of Christianity still alive and growing fifty years from now. Still, there is a great deal of confusion about Pentecostalism. Those whose thinking has been wholly molded by scientism and rationalism are more than skeptical about this movement. Some pseudosophisticates in mainline churches shake their heads in disbelief that so many, in their judgment, have been "taken in" by the emotional appeals of Pentecostalism. Others wonder why Pentecostalism thrives, especially after the falls from grace of Jimmy Swaggart and Jim Bakker, two of the movement's most famous TV personalities. But thrive it does! To understand Pentecostalism fully, you must take into account its origins and its influence in America and around the world.

The Pentecostal movement erupted in the early part of the twentieth century in many different places, but its origins can be traced back to a humble house on Bonnie Brae Street in Los Angeles on the evening of April 9, 1906. A handful of Christians had been praying for a special "breakthrough" from God—and on that night, it happened. Some of the men and women at the gathering suddenly experienced an unusual infilling of the Holy Spirit that had them praying in tongues and creating a loving community that transcended lines of race and social class. In an era of great division, such interracial and interclass interaction was nothing short of miraculous.

News spread like wildfire of the special blessing from God that was given to the Christians at that prayer meeting. Soon, people were coming from all over the Los Angeles area to get a glimpse of this incredible spiritual revival. Given the prevailing racism of the time, the fact that black people, Latino people, white people, poor people, and rich people were all coming together—worshipping together and hugging one another—was even more startling to onlookers than the phenomena of Christians speaking in tongues. As the number of people attending these prayer meetings continued to grow, the meetings were soon moved to an old, abandoned Methodist church on Azusa Street. From there, the movement spread around the world. At first, it drew people from beaten-down socioeconomic classes; they found a sense of empowerment in the spiritual ecstasies that often accompanied their being "filled with the Holy Spirit." But it wasn't long before economically successful people began to recognize God's presence in Pentecostal Christians and to believe in the authenticity of their claims of spiritual experiences like those of first-century Christians on the day of Pentecost. You may recall the story as recorded in Acts II. It says there that when the Holy Spirit came upon the church, the people spoke in tongues, prophesied, and adopted lifestyles that involved sacrificially sharing their financial resources.

First, let me tell you that there is a difference between *speaking* in tongues and *praying* in tongues. It is the latter that is most common in Pentecostal meetings. Praying in tongues is one expression of what the apostle Paul was referring to in Romans 8:26–27 when he wrote that we do not know how to pray as we ought, but the Holy Spirit intercedes and, through inarticulate groanings, pleads for us to God. Pentecostals believe the strange sounds that they utter when praying in tongues are unintelligible to human ears, but God knows the longings of their hearts and exactly what they mean and need. There are times when praising God fills Pentecostal Christians with such intense emotion that human language cannot provide the means to articulate it. That is when, they believe, the Holy Spirit prays through them with utterances that only God can understand. These feelings, they say, transcend the categories of understanding of this world's cultures, and so the languages of these cultures cannot give expression to them. Pentecostals will tell you that the Holy Spirit gives "heavenly languages" unique to each individual to provide the means for full and free prayerful worship of God.

While I am not into praying in tongues myself, I fully believe in its validity. However, some other Evangelicals, especially Fundamentalists such as Southern Baptists, disagree with me and strongly oppose the practice. Anti-Pentecostal Fundamentalists believe that praying in tongues is something that was okay in the early church, but that such "gifts of the Holy Spirit" came to an end when the canon of the New Testament was completed. They quote I Corinthians 13, which reads, "where there are prophecies, they will cease; where there are tongues, they will be stilled; where there is knowledge, it will pass away. For we know in part and we prophesy in part, but when perfection comes, the imperfect disappears."

Claiming that the "perfection" referred to in this verse is the text of the New Testament, they say that anything having to do with praying or speaking in tongues should have ceased after the church had these writings. Consequently, they say, "the gift of tongues" in these present days is, at best, nothing more than emotionalism—and, at worst, a demonic means of diminishing the importance of the New Testament. Personally, I think that this judgment, which relies on a flimsy biblical basis, is stretching things a bit far. But Southern Baptist Fundamentalists will not tolerate anything having to do with tongues in their fellowship. One of the top executives in the Southern Baptist Convention has been severely attacked and has had his job threatened because he admitted to praying in tongues *in private*.

Speaking in tongues is quite another thing. It is not to be confused with praying in tongues. This particular practice, according to what Paul writes in 1 Corinthians 12:10, is a unique gift that God gives to certain people so that, through them, God can offer special truths to the church. Paul writes, "Now to each one the manifestation of the Spirit is given for the common good. To one there is given through the Spirit the message of wisdom, to another the message of knowledge by means of the same Spirit, to another faith by the same Spirit, to another gifts of healing by that one Spirit, to another miraculous powers, to another prophecy, to another distinguishing between spirits, to another speaking in different kinds of tongues, and to still another the interpretation of tongues. All these are the work of one and the same Spirit, and he gives them to each one, just as he determines."

While all can *pray* in tongues, according to the Pentecostals, only those with a unique gift from God can *speak* in tongues. When someone speaks in tongues, he or she is in some kind of trance and may not be fully conscious of what is happening. If the congregation is to receive a message from God through this speaking in tongues, then there must be someone present who has the gift of interpretation. Paul wrote in 1 Corinthians 14:27–28 that it is best for a person with the gift of speaking in tongues to keep silent if there is no one present to interpret the message, since such speech will only lead to confusion.

Pentecostal Christians also believe in the other spiritual gifts described in 1 Corinthians 12, including the gifts of prophecy, preaching, faith, healing, and spiritual discernment. The scope of this book does not allow me to explain how each of these gifts functions in the life of the church. Let me assure you, however, that there is a biblical basis for the claim that these gifts should be practiced in the twenty-first-century church just as they were in the first-century church. The purpose of these gifts, according to Scripture, is to help other Christians in the church grow in their love for Christ and in their understanding of what God wants them to be and do. Pentecostal Christians believe that the use of these gifts empowers the church to more effectively spread the salvation message and work for peace and justice. I affirm what Pentecostals teach about the gifts of the Holy Spirit, and contend that what they teach is validated by Scripture. I'm not sure where you two will come out on this matter, but I hope you'll be cautious. Remember, Jesus once said that whoever slanders the work of the Holy Spirit is in danger of eternal damnation (Mark 3:29).

Don't be intimidated by Pentecostalism on the basis that you don't pray in tongues or are not aware of possessing any of the gifts of the Spirit. While some Pentecostals put an undue emphasis on exercising "spiritual gifts" and see the gift of tongues as a sign of whether a person is filled with the Holy Spirit, the Bible does not. These days, most Pentecostals recognize that in Scripture spirituality is determined not by whether you can exercise the gifts of the Holy Spirit but by whether your life gives evidence of the fruits of the Spirit. The Bible says that it is by our fruits that we shall be known, not by our gifts. The fruits of the Spirit, as listed in Galatians 5:22–23, are love, joy, peace, patience, kindness, goodness, fidelity, gentleness, and self-control. The more the Holy Spirit permeates your personality, the more these traits and qualities will be evident in your life. Furthermore, the apostle Paul concludes his discussion of the gifts of the Spirit in 1 Corinthians 12 by declaring that there is something better than any of these gifts. In the following chapter, he declares that it is most important to express the ultimate fruit of Spirit, which is love. In 1 Corinthians 13, one of his most well-known writings, Paul declares that if he speaks in tongues but doesn't live out love, he's just making a lot of noise. He insists that no spiritual gift—whether it be the gift of prophecy, or the gift of knowledge, or the gift of faith—is worth anything without love.

Whatever you may think about Pentecostal religious practices, you must understand that Pentecostalism is not some sectarian movement that other Christians can ignore. It is a dominating presence in the larger Evangelical world, and it even has made significant inroads into mainline denominational churches. In 1960, Dennis Bennett, rector of St. Mark's Episcopal Church in Los Angeles, brought Pentecostalism into the Anglican tradition. David Runnion-Bareford leads Focus Renewal, a Pentecostal movement within the United Church of Christ. A group called Presbyterian Reformed Ministries International is bringing Pentecostalism into the Presbyterian tradition.

Even the Roman Catholics have been touched by this movement. On an airplane trip some twenty years ago, I was somewhat surprised to find myself surrounded by a group of Pentecostal Catholics. Some of them were priests and nuns, but most were laypersons. These Christians were having a great time as they laughed, joked, and sang praise songs together. I hadn't been with a group that spiritually energetic since my teenage days at summer youth camp. I couldn't help but get into the spirit of things and join in with their singing. When I asked where they were going, a priest told me, "We're a bunch of Holy Spirit–filled Catholics on our way to Notre Dame University for a renewal conference, and we can't help but sing praises to the Lord."

Pentecostals in mainline denominational churches usually adopt a somewhat more sophisticated label and call themselves "charismatic Christians." But the only real difference between those who call themselves Pentecostals and those who call themselves charismatic Christians is that the latter tend to be people with higher incomes and more formal education than the former.

The most significant way in which Pentecostalism has impacted mainline denominational churches has been through its innovations in worship. The "praise music" of Pentecostalism is becoming standard in almost every kind of church. Praise bands with guitars and drums are replacing organs in worship services everywhere. A whole new genre of music that has come out of Pentecostalism is invading mainline denominational churches.

Chuck Smith, pastor of Calvary Chapel in Costa Mesa, California, and one of the primary leaders of the Jesus People Movement during the late 1960s and early

1970s, got the craze for worship music going when he produced a record of praise music back in 1971. The album sold hundreds of thousands of copies and led to the creation of Maranatha Music, a leader in the now multi-million-dollar contemporary-Christian-music industry. In the United Kingdom, Graham Kendrick and the band Delirious gave the British their own special brand of praise music. And in Australia, the Hillsong Church became an international center for training Christians to be worship leaders in churches that embrace this new music. Whether you go into a small-town Evangelical church, a suburban mega-church, or a mainline denominational church, you are likely to hear the same kind of music performed in pretty much the same way. There is a similar style and feel to praise music, regardless of the congregation.

The rise of this new worship music has led to what some call "the worship wars." Traditionalists who prefer the old hymns by the likes of the Wesleys and Fanny Crosby often react strongly against this new music and the style of worship associated with it, which they criticize as "planned spontaneity." Many churches have split over these worship wars, but the majority have made adjustments to include people on both sides. Some have accommodated to praise music and the kind of worship that accompanies it by holding "blended services" that incorporate both praise music and traditional hymns. Others have set aside a special hour for what they call a "contemporary worship service," in addition to their more traditional worship service.

I imagine that you two are enthusiastic fans of this new worship music. Most young Evangelicals are. To be honest, old-timers like me have a hard time with it. I find the constant repetition of words that is typical in this music somewhat irritating. I sometimes joke that the only difference I can find between the new worship music and a machine gun is that a machine gun only has a hundred rounds. I like singing old, familiar hymns from a hymn book, and if I get to Heaven and find an overhead projector displaying praise-music lyrics instead of a traditional hymnal, I'm checking out!

But however I feel about this new praise music, I am completely in favor of it because of how it affects young people like you. I've never seen anything like the way teenagers and young adults gravitate to the new styles of worship that employ this music. I've already mentioned how young people flock to the voluntary chapel services at Eastern University, where I've taught for forty years, primarily because of the exuberant singing and Pentecostal-like worship. Joe Modica, our university chaplain, has a Pentecostal background. When he came to Eastern, he recast our chapel services with a more Pentecostal feel. To say that our students enjoy the chapel services is an understatement. When I look around and see their closed eyes, their upraised hands, and the ecstasy on their faces as they sing praise songs, I have to admit that I never found worship so meaningful when I was their age. I've learned from Bob Dylan not to criticize what I don't understand, "'cause the times, they are a-changin'."

Howard Goss, one of the foremost leaders of Pentecostalism, has contended that, without this music, the Pentecostal movement could never have made such rapid inroads into the hearts of men and women. And it has also injected some new life into mainline Christianity, and alleviated what many young people consider to be the dullness of traditional worship.

In Matthew 13:52, Jesus says that every scribe in God's kingdom is like a householder who opens a treasure chest and out of it takes some things new and some things old. Jesus understood balance, and I hope we can all learn from him. The kingdom of God will not exclusively feature new music or traditional music. There has to be room for both. That is why I appreciate those blended worship services that incorporate both new praise music and old, beloved hymns.

So far, I've given you such a glowing picture of Pentecostalism that you might get the impression that the movement is all light and sunshine. That is not the case. There is a downside to Pentecostalism, and you should be aware of that. This movement is conditioning the future of all of Evangelicalism, and we have to defend ourselves against certain un-Christian and destructive propensities within it.

One of the most objectionable tendencies I find in Pentecostalism is its frequent embrace of what is called "prosperity theology." This theology erroneously promises that if you live right and pray right, you'll prosper materially. I don't want to give the impression that prosperity theology pervades Pentecostalism, but there are far too many preachers in this movement who seem to be saying that if you make Jesus your choice, you'll drive a Rolls-Royce. Prosperity theology is based on the premise that as a child of the King of Kings "who owns the cattle on a thousand hills and the wealth of every mine," in the words of the old hymn, you are destined to be heir to his riches. Expensive cars, thousand-dollar suits, and mansion-like houses are cited as evidence of how God blesses the faithful.

The Old Testament lends some support to this idea. In ancient Israel, whenever the people were right with God, they prospered, and whenever they were out of touch with the Almighty, they suffered from famine and conquests by enemy nations. That is why Job was bewildered when calamities came his way. Since he had lived righteously before God, he couldn't understand why bad things happened to him. Job thought that righteousness should be rewarded in this life. This belief was especially held in Bible days among Orthodox Jews such as the Sadducees, who did not believe in an afterlife.

But prosperity-theology preachers should recognize that Jesus never promised his followers good health and big bank accounts. In Matthew 8:20, Jesus warns that "the foxes have their holes and the birds have their nests; but the Son of Man has nowhere to lay his head." He let it be known that servants are not better off than their masters: since he was a man of sorrows and grief, they should expect to be the same. Consider the fact that all of the apostles suffered privation and, except for John, died as martyrs. Also, think of all the Christians in Third World countries who endure great poverty in spite of their faithfulness.

According to the New Testament, there isn't anything wrong with earning a million dollars—but there *is* something wrong with keeping it. 1 John 3:17–18 asks, If we have the good things of this world and fail to share with a brother or sister in need, how can it be said that we have the love of God in our hearts?

What I find especially reprehensible are those televangelist rip-off artists who prey on folks with limited incomes, telling them that if they send in money for the preacher's ministries (a large proportion of which goes to line the evangelist's own pocket), then God will reward them by giving them back tenfold the amount of their contributions. This same kind of prosperity preaching is rampant among Pentecostals in developing nations. In Africa, tens of thousands of people in megachurches make sacrifices that they can ill afford, hoping that God will reward their faithfulness, while their gifts finance the affluent lifestyles of some Pentecostal preachers. Responsible leaders of large Pentecostal denominations must come out loud and clear against this kind of preaching.

Prosperity theology isn't the only serious problem in Pentecostalism. Another is some preachers' exaggerations of the healings that occur in Pentecostal churches and Gospel crusades—exaggerations that are often accepted without question by the people in attendance. While the tendency to exaggerate about such things to aggrandize their ministries is not unique to Pentecostal preachers, it is most common among them. Don't get me wrong! I believe in healings. Miracles are not a thing of the past. They are happening today. But I have heard too many stories of supposed miracles that, upon investigation, are revealed as gross exaggerations of reality. God doesn't need lies to establish credibility. Where false claims about miracles are exposed, as they often are, cynicism about Christianity grows.

One time, against my better judgment, I was a guest on *The 700 Club*, one of America's most famous Christian television shows. Another of host Pat Robertson's guests that day was a man from Romania who claimed that he once had been dead for twenty-four hours, after which Jesus brought him back to life. This guest reported that he had gone to Hell, where devils poked at him with pitchforks while he suffered the torments of the flames. I wasn't on the set during that segment of the show. If I had been, I would have questioned the veracity of the story. That Pat Robertson didn't challenge the man really ticked me off. He should not have allowed a story like that to go out over the airwaves worldwide without calling the man's story into question.

To make matters worse, that was the same show on which Pat Robertson prayed a hurricane away from Virginia Beach—or so he claimed. A hurricane was coming up the Atlantic seaboard toward Virginia Beach, where Robertson's television station is located, but Robertson prayed that the station would be spared from the effects of the storm. He later claimed that, because of his prayers, God turned the hurricane away from Virginia Beach and the TV station was spared.

What upsets me about stories like that is what they suggest about those who *do* experience tragedies. What are we saying about poor people such as those in the New Orleans's Ninth Ward who were victimized by Katrina? The implication is that if they had been as spiritual as Pat Robertson is, they would have been delivered from the wrath of that storm. The fact that they suffered destruction from a hurricane would seem to be evidence of their spiritual inferiority to Robertson, whose prayers were apparently more effective.

I believe in healings. I know people who have been miraculously cured of cancer because of prayer. James 5:14 says that if a person is sick, the elders of the church should be called to anoint that person with oil and pray for his healing. I have seen that done, and I know people who have been healed that way. But too many Pentecostal preachers act like they can guarantee healings, and give reports of such spectacular results that I know they are wildly exaggerating and, in some cases, outright lying. What's worse is that those who aren't healed at the hands of such Pentecostal healers are then blamed for their lack of faith. If that's not adding insult to injury, I don't know what is.

My final concern about Pentecostalism is perhaps the most serious. Too often, I see the faith hijacked by cults of personality. Certain healers and preachers are viewed as larger-than-life supersaints whose powers make them superior to other Christians. Although these leaders may not always seek such elite status, the adherents of the movement regularly attribute such status to them.

The dangers of being put on a pedestal are all too evident. Consider what happened to both Jim Bakker and Jimmy Swaggart. I am convinced that these men were not evil. But when they were treated as if they were in a special category of super-Christians, it was easy for them to be seduced into thinking that they were not subject to the same rules as everybody else. What's worse is that such religious superstars rarely are held accountable by their peers. Their financial practices and sex lives are seldom questioned. Such idolization sets a person up for a disastrous fall. It is no surprise, therefore, that the religious landscape is littered with fallen Pentecostal preachers. However, don't think for one moment that it's only

Pentecostal preachers who are vulnerable to the destructive effects of the cult of personality. The problem is evident throughout the Evangelical community, and you must be careful to avoid this kind of seduction.

Despite all of its weaknesses and shortcomings, I still feel that the Pentecostal movement is the best thing that has happened to the church in centuries. The rationalistic theologies of both modernism and Fundamentalism had left the world with an ecstasy deficit, and Pentecostalism has done much to remedy that deficiency.

I'll have to say more about being filled with the Holy Spirit in another letter. For now, let me tell you both that it is more than possible to be a Pentecostal without speaking in tongues, if by "Pentecostal" we mean one who is filled with the same Holy Spirit that fell upon the church on the first Pentecost almost two thousand years ago. The best evidence of our being filled with the Holy Spirit is the way the fruits of the Spirit are expressed in our everyday lives. That's really what Pentecostalism, at its best, is all about.

Sincerely,
Tony

8

■ History with a Happy Ending

Dear Junia and Timothy,

There's a lot of talk these days about the coming end of the world as we know it. Major newspapers, magazines, and television news programs are featuring stories that ask whether Armageddon, the battle that many Christians believe will precede the Second Coming of Christ, is at hand. Certainly, recent events in the Middle East have prompted a lot of people who aren't particularly religious to wonder if those strange people carrying sandwich boards that read REPENT! THE END IS NEAR! might know something that they don't. The sale of 70 million copies of the *Left Behind* books gives ample evidence that the Second Coming of Christ is on the minds of people everywhere.

Theologians and Bible scholars refer to the study of the way that history will come to an end as "eschatology." I have to tell you that there is no unanimity on this subject among Evangelicals. While all of us agree that

Jesus will one day return—in accordance with the Apostles' Creed—how, why, and when is up for serious debate within our faith community.

It should be enough to say that if you read the Bible, you will know how history will end—we will win! Certainly, we sing about such a climactic telos in the "Hallelujah Chorus" of Handel's *Messiah*. Those wonderful words of hope drawn from the book of Revelation are heard at Easter and Christmas in churches all across the country.

> *The kingdoms of this world are become the kingdoms of our Lord, and of his Christ;*
> *and he shall reign for ever and ever . . . Hallelujah!*

That inspiring statement is part of the reason why Evangelicals' message to the rest of the world is known as "the Gospel"—the word *gospel* is derived from a Greek word that translates literally as "good news." The coming of the kingdom of God is good news. The Bible is filled with hope. It tells us that, in the midst of all the evils and discouragements that we encounter in this world, God is working to bring about the ultimate good that was planned for this world when it was created (Romans 8:28).

The crucifixion and resurrection of Jesus assure us that Christ is alive and well and cannot be defeated by the diabolical powers that seem to be everywhere at work in the world. If ever the forces of evil were going to gain the upper hand in their cosmic struggle with God, it would have been when Jesus was nailed to Calvary's cross. That was when the God who was in Christ was the most vulnerable. It looked really bleak that afternoon, when the dying Jesus cried out, "It is finished!" and surrendered to death. For three days, despair prevailed among believers and angels alike. Then, on the third day, to the amazement of all, the powers of darkness were overcome. You know what happened next. As the Easter hymn declares,

> Up from the grave he arose,
> with a mighty triumph o'er his foes.
> He arose a victor from the dark domain,
> and he lives forever with his saints to reign.

In every war there is a decisive battle that spells the inevitable defeat of the enemy. In the Napoleonic Wars it was Waterloo. In the U.S. Civil War it was Gettysburg. And in World War II it was D-day—the day the American troops and their allies established a beachhead on the shores of Normandy. After each of these crucial battles, there could be no doubt as to how the war would end. Yet those wars did not end immediately after those battles. In fact, there was more suffering, death, and destruction between D-day and V-day (the day World War II ended) than at any other time during that war.

The death and resurrection of Jesus was God's D-day. It was the decisive battle that determined the outcome of history. All the forces that the Evil One could muster were unified against Christ in what proved to be the decisive cosmic struggle between the forces of light and the forces of darkness. When that battle was over it was Christus Victor.

But demonic forces are still at work in the world. Between God's D-day and God's V-day—that future time when all evil will be subdued and God's kingdom will be fully established on earth—there has been and will be suffering, destruction, and death. Each generation continues the struggle to completely overcome the forces of evil. We live with the challenge to join in God's efforts to change the world, and we do so with the assurance of the eventual triumph of God and actualization of the kingdom of righteousness.

The eschatology of the Bible could not be clearer. It is not just the "Hallelujah Chorus" of Handel's *Messiah* that promises that the kingdoms of this world will become the kingdom of our God as recorded in Revelations. Jesus himself explains how the kingdom of God will develop within history in two of his most well-known parables. In Matthew 13:31–33, he said,

> *"The kingdom of heaven is like a mustard seed, which a man took and planted in his field. Though it is the smallest of all your seeds, yet when it grows, it is the*

largest of garden plants and becomes a tree, so that the birds of the air come and perch in its branches."

He told them still another parable: "The kingdom of heaven is like yeast that a woman took and mixed into a large amount of flour until it worked all through the dough."

With such optimistic prophecies, it is surprising that many Christians do not believe that the Bible's message is hopeful. I remember sitting in church as a boy and listening to the preacher explain that the world was in a spiritually downward spiral into corruption and destruction. He described increasing sexual immorality and crime, and decreasing church membership. He warned that Christians should expect increasing persecution. While the preacher went on and on with his litany of bad news, a woman sitting behind me muttered softly, "The signs of the times! Thank you, Jesus! Praise be to God."

I asked my mother why the woman was so happy about what she was hearing from the pulpit. My mother answered, "She is happy because she's hearing how the world is getting worse and worse, and she believes that if things get perverted and messed up enough, Jesus will return. What the preacher is saying is convincing her that things are so bad right now that Jesus's Second Coming must be at hand. That's why she's pleased with what she's hearing."

What that woman was thinking was half-true. Evil *is* on the increase. There are stories of the social and moral disintegration of society on the front page of almost any newspaper on almost any day. But don't get discouraged by the reality that "there will be wars and rumors of wars" (Matthew 24:6) and "the poor you will have with you always" (Mark 14:7) right up until Christ's return. Don't be dismayed that truth seems always on the scaffold while evil seems to sit firmly on the throne. As a great hymn tells us,

> *Yet that scaffold sways the future,*
> *And behind the dim unknown,*
> *Standeth God within the shadow*
> *Keeping watch above his own.*

Be aware that as the kingdom of evil grows daily, so does the kingdom of God. Right alongside the manifestations of the kingdom of evil, the kingdom of God also is manifest—and it, too, is becoming more evident every day.

Jesus gives this parable in Matthew 13:24–30:

> *The kingdom of heaven is likened unto a man which sowed good seed in his field: But while men slept, his enemy came and sowed tares among the wheat, and went his way. But when the blade was sprung up, and brought forth fruit, then appeared the tares also. So*

*the servants of the householder came and said unto
him, "Sir, didst not thou sow good seed in thy field?
from whence then hath it tares?" He said unto them,
"An enemy hath done this." The servants said unto
him, "Wilt thou then that we go and gather them
up?" But he said, "Nay; lest while ye gather up the
tares, ye root up also the wheat with them. Let both
grow together until the harvest: and in the time of
harvest I will say to the reapers, 'Gather ye together
first the tares, and bind them in bundles to burn
them: but gather the wheat into my barn.'"*

The meaning of Jesus's words is obvious. The tares
symbolize manifestations of the kingdom of evil, and the
wheat symbolizes manifestations of the kingdom of God.
In this parable, Jesus was telling his disciples that both
the kingdom of evil *and* the kingdom of God will flourish and intensify right up until the end. Then, he assures
them, the kingdom of evil will be totally destroyed.

History provides evidence that both kingdoms are on
the increase. On the one hand, evil has never been more
powerful and prevalent than it is today—but neither has
God's kingdom. Here in the United States as well as in
Western Europe, we may feel that the church is in decline and obscenity is growing ever more evident. But
don't get so blinded by what is happening in your immediate surroundings that you fail to recognize what is
happening in the rest of the world. In Latin America,

Africa, and Asia, the church is growing by leaps and bounds. In Africa alone, more than 50,000 new converts are joining the church every week.

There are many other signs of the growth of God's kingdom. Surprising as it may be, social conditions are improving in many parts of the world. In the last ten years, infant deaths caused by hunger and malnutrition have decreased, while literacy rates and the percentage of the earth's population with access to clean drinking water have increased. Polio and smallpox have almost been wiped out. True, there are new evils in the world, such as a growing global AIDS epidemic. But don't lose sight of the good that is happening. The church will not limp out of history battered and beaten. It will march out of history in triumph. One day—some day—a trumpet will sound, and the Lord will return, and all evil will be abolished, and all demonic forces will be subdued. And then the world will be as it should be.

Given all of this good news about the end of history, how did that woman in my church get the idea that everything in the world was getting worse and worse, that righteousness was declining, and that this bad news was evidence that Jesus would soon come again? The answer is that she, like a good proportion of the Evangelical community, had been seduced by the eschatology of John Nelson Darby. That is a name you should remember.

John Nelson Darby was an Anglican priest living in the city of Plymouth, England, in the early part of the nineteenth century. Disenchanted with the Anglican Church, he broke with his denomination and started a new religious movement called the Plymouth Brethren. Darby and his followers in this movement propagated a new theology known as dispensationalism, which introduced a brand-new idea into Evangelical theology: "the rapture." What he taught about the rapture generated dark and dismal expectations for the future among many Evangelicals, including that woman in my church.

Darby believed that the world will become more and more degenerate until Christ returns. But he did not believe that Christ will return "all the way" and touch down on the earth. Instead, contended Darby, Christ will "rapture" *out* of the world all true Christians to meet him "in the air," leaving apostate Christians and nonbelievers behind to endure a seven-year period of incredible "tribulation and suffering." After that, according to Darby's dispensationalist theology, Christ will return again, establish his kingdom on earth, and send all who are not true Christians into the "lake of fire." The word *rapture* does not appear in the Bible. It was invented by Darby. That is not to say that the doctrine does not have biblical support. The passage most commonly cited to undergird belief in a rapture is I Thessalonians 4:16–17:

Then we which are alive and remain shall be caught up together with them in the clouds, to meet the Lord in the air; and so shall we ever be with the Lord.

Those of us who reject Darby's invention of the rapture believe that Paul wrote these words to comfort the early Christians who were concerned that those believers who were already dead when Christ returned would not participate in the joys of the Second Coming. He comforts them with the assurance that they will be the first to share in this incredible event. The word that he uses for "meet" in this passage is the Greek word *apantesis*, which was used to describe citizens' going to meet a visiting dignitary to escort him into their city. Paul is comforting the Thessalonian Christians with the good news that those who have died will be the first to join Christ upon his return, and that living Christians will join them in accompanying Christ on his journey to earth to set up God's kingdom. That is certainly what is suggested earlier, in verse 14, which reads,

For if we believe that Jesus died and rose again, even so them which sleep in Jesus will God bring with him.

This interpretation of what happens at the secomd coming of Christ, with which I agree, is far different than the dispensationalist's concept of the rapture. According to dispensationalist theology, Jesus never really touches down to earth at his second coming, but only comes to rescue out of the world true Christians, saving them for the coming seven years of what they call "the great Tribulation." Only after that, say the Darbyites, does Jesus come all the way back to earth. Following what is really his third return does he imprison Satan and all of Satan's agents, and reigns over the earth for one thousand years. The elaborate eschatological scheme, invented by John Nelson Darby and propagated by the Plymouth Brethren, had never before existed in the history of the church. None of the great theologians of the past—including Augustine, Thomas Aquinas, Ulrich Zwingli, Martin Luther, John Calvin, and John Wesley—even hinted at such an eschatology. All of these great theologians believed that Jesus would return one day to join the church here on earth, triumph over evil, and establish God's kingdom in this world.

This, of course, raises the obvious question as to how Darby's eschatology has become almost normative among contemporary Evangelicals. Why is it that, if you were in a room with a thousand Evangelical Christians and asked, "How many of you believe in the rapture?" nearly every hand would go up? The answer is the Scofield Reference Bible.

Back in 1907, Oxford University Press began publishing this text, which was was written by the amateur theologian Cyrus Ingerson Scofield. Tutored by the Reverend

James H. Brookes, who was known as the father of American dispensationalism, Scofield sought to propagate Darbyite ideas to the broadest possible audience.

The Scofield Reference Bible was innovative in that the top of each page contained Scripture, and the bottom was dedicated to commentary. It was in this commentary that Darbyites such as Scofield gave their rapture theology to the rest of the Evangelical community. There is no way to underestimate the role that this study Bible has played in shaping the way some Evangelicals, and especially Fundamentalists, think about the Second Coming of Christ. All across America, there are Bible colleges that have organized curriculums around the teachings in the Scofield Reference Bible. Vast numbers of preachers and teachers in America's churches are graduates of these schools.

Scofield's study Bible became a best seller; even today, the folks at Oxford University Press will tell you that it earns more money for their company than any other single publication. As a young man, I owned a copy of the Scofield Reference Bible, and I was convinced that the reference notes at the bottom of the pages were almost as much inspired by the Holy Spirit as the text of the Scripture at the top of the pages.

More recently, the doctrine of the rapture has had an almost unchallenged boost from the best-selling *Left Behind* books written by Tim LaHaye, a prominent televangelist, and Jerry B. Jenkins, a popular Christian writer.

The *Left Behind* books are now available in just about every bookstore in America. With more than 70 million copies sold worldwide, they outsell the books of popular authors such as Stephen King and John Grisham. The *Left Behind* books describe what the rapture might be like if it occurs in the immediate future. Automobiles crash because Christian drivers are suddenly caught up to meet Christ "in the air"; scores of people suddenly disappear from shopping malls; and a host of other shocking things occur. The books are fascinating adventure stories that make for good entertainment, but they also make Darby's theology seem realistic and tenable. Their influence on American Evangelical thinking has been enormous. Nowadays, to even question Darby's theology as presented by LaHaye and Jenkins is to be deemed a heretic in many, if not most, Evangelical circles.

Maybe you are thinking, "So what? Why is it a big deal that this innovation in Evangelical theology has become commonplace among our people? What harm can it do?"

In response to such questions, I have to answer emphatically, "A great deal of harm!"

According to Darby and his successors, the period leading up to the rapture will be characterized *solely* by the disintegration of good, growing apostasy in the churches, and the emergence of a totalitarian world government legitimized by apostate churches— in other words, by the expansion of the kingdom of evil.

There is nothing in dispensationalism about the increase of the kingdom of God leading up to the eschaton—and I believe that this contradicts the Bible, which predicts increasing manifestations of God's kingdom during this time.

The implication of dispensationalism is that there is no point to working toward peace, social justice, the end of poverty, and the like, on the basis that such projects are ultimately futile. John Nelson Darby, Tim LaHaye, Jerry Jenkins all emphasize that the church should not engage in such tasks. The church, they say, should concentrate all of its efforts on one thing—getting people "saved." Converting people so that they are ready for the rapture is all that matters to them. They argue that preachers who call the church to work for justice on behalf of the poor and oppressed are, at best, wasting their time and, at worst, leading people into erroneous secular humanism. They argue that social-gospel preachers can be accused, whether they realize it or not, of being agents of the anti-Christ.

Dispensationalism thus justifies the repudiation of the United Nations and any other body that tries to unite nations in a quest for world peace. According to the dispensationalist view, such bodies are organizational instruments through which the anti-Christ can exercise his evil control over the earth. This is why many Christians in the Evangelical community are opposed to the United Nations and cheer on politicians who want to pull the United States out of the organization. Some extremists oppose even the collection of money for starving children through the UNICEF program, claiming that this, too, is part of Satan's plan. This theology has turned many Evangelicals into conspiracy theorists who are convinced that any such efforts are covert parts of a diabolical plot.

Finally, dispensationalist theology, with its rapture doctrine, has become the ideological basis for an Evangelical Zionist movement that seriously endangers relations between the West and the Islamic world. According to those in the Darby school of thought, the Jews must become the sole inhabitants of the Holy Land before Christ can return. The dispensationalist interpretation of biblical prophecy holds that the Second Coming of Christ is contingent on exclusive possession by the children of Israel of the land promised to Abraham's seed in Genesis 12. For this to occur, all Arab peoples now living in Israel and Palestine would have to leave the Holy Land, either freely or by force. In the "end times," Evangelical Zionists believe, the Jews, who will then solely occupy the land, will receive the Gospel and be converted to Christianity, or themselves experience the wrath of God.

Recently, I was on a radio talk show with an Evangelical Zionist, and I asked him what he thought should be done with the Arab peoples in the Holy Land if they resist removal. The man answered, "Then they will have to be killed!" When I expressed shocked horror at his proposal, he pointed out that when the ancient Jews were led into the Holy Land by Joshua, all the inhabitants of the land were systematically put to death—and he believes that this might have to happen again. When I suggested that what he was proposing was ethnic cleansing, he responded by saying that, in this case, ethnic cleansing would be God's will.

In case you may think such thinking is restricted to a handful of oddballs, I suggest that you ask around and find out for yourselves how many Evangelicals you talk to hold to such dangerous ideas. They are far more common than you might think.

Unfortunately, Evangelical Zionists forget a couple of salient facts. Foremost is that the Arab peoples are also the seed of Abraham. Given that reality, aren't the Arabs every bit as entitled to the land as are the Jews?

The second is that the land promised to the seed of Abraham stretches from the Euphrates River to the Nile. According to the beliefs of Evangelical Zionists, all of this land should be exclusively in the hands of the Jews. This would mean that all Arab peoples would have to be driven out of Lebanon, a good part of Syria, and a significant part of what is now Egypt. The ramifications, should the Evangelical Zionists have their way, are extremely frightening.

While I don't think this particular land grab is likely to be pursued, I do think that Evangelical Zionists, inspired by the eschatology of Darby and his modern-day proponents, could push successfully for policies in the Middle East that would have dire consequences for the entire world. Already, Evangelical Zionists such as televangelist Pat Robertson have such a large following that the people in the White House cannot ignore their vision for the future of Israel. When Israeli Prime Minister Ariel Sharon unilaterally closed down Jewish settlements in the Gaza strip and ordered the land turned over to Palestinians, Evangelical Zionists let the politicians in Washington know of their displeasure and proclaimed that such action was in opposition to God's will. Leaders of the Evangelical Zionist movement have also let it be known that withdrawal from the West Bank area adjacent to the Jordan River would be, in their estimation, intolerable.

The influence of Evangelical Zionists is dramatically evident in America's handling of the Palestinian-Israeli conflict. Under pressure from these Evangelicals, the United States has done little more than offer weak objections while Israel has driven Palestinians off land they've lived on for years, bulldozed their homes, and built hundreds of Jewish settlements on that land. Evangelical Zionists did nothing to oppose this, despite the fact that about 15 percent of the Arabs on this land were Christians. These Arab Christians were more than dismayed that their Evangelical brothers and sisters in America were indifferent to the injustices being heaped upon them. Palestinians could do little while this land grab was being carried out by Israel's army, which is the fourth most powerful in the world.

Arabs and other Muslims are well aware that Israel's military power is mostly paid for with U.S. tax dollars. They note that one-quarter of all foreign aid given away by the United States each year goes to Israel, and that this aid is what enables Israel to build and maintain its powerful army. And so the net result of Evangelical Zionist–supported U.S. policies is that the entire Muslim world views the ill treatment of Palestinians as actions taken by an Israeli-American coalition. As you can well imagine, this view is widely exploited by terrorist groups such as Al-Qaeda for propaganda purposes. It follows that there is a growing hostility among Muslims toward America because of what they perceive to be massive, one-sided support of Zionism. This hostility has been exacerbated by irresponsible statements made by some of our most well-known Evangelical leaders. You may have heard their incendiary comments denigrating both Muhammad and the Islamic religion on Christian radio and television shows. Many scholars and pundits have predicted that the twenty-first century will be defined by massive wars between Muslim nations and the so-called Christian nations. Evangelical Zionists may well be contributing to the fulfillment of this prophecy.

Ironically, Jewish Zionists are just beginning to grasp the threat these Evangelical Zionists pose for the future of Israel. Jewish Zionists are committed to having a homeland with secure borders for their people, but they realize that a few million Jews in the Holy Land will never have any true security unless they are at peace with the 50 million Arabs in the adjacent countries that surround them. They are becoming increasingly aware that the Evangelical Zionists and their extremist views may prevent that peace.

I'm amazed at how few outsiders recognize the extent to which an eschatology stemming from a nineteenth-century British cleric has influenced our nation's domestic and foreign policies. On the domestic scene, consider how former secretary of the Interior James Watt, a dispensationalist Evangelical, proposed plans that could have destructively exploited oil and other natural resources in our national parks and forests. He advocated this policy because he believed that Jesus would soon return, so there was no need to protect those resources for future generations. When it comes to foreign affairs, consider that former president Ronald Reagan was reportedly convinced by Jerry Falwell that the Battle of Armageddon was about to happen. Under the influence of Falwell's dispensationalist theology, the president was convinced that the army of the anti-Christ in this imminent battle was that of the Soviet Union, and that God's army was that of America. For Reagan, that made expanding the U.S. military a religious obligation. President Reagan was led to believe that only a highly equipped military, armed with an overload of atomic weaponry, would be able to overcome the onslaught of the Evil One in the coming "last days." The influence of modern-day versions of Darby's eschatology continues to increase as Evangelicals who espouse that theology gain power. It poses a danger that cannot be ignored.

I, like most Christians raised on Darby's eschatology, had little idea of the political implications of this kind of thinking. The mainline denominational church I belonged to gave almost no attention to eschatology and left me with a sense that dispensationalism, with its particular doctrine of what leads up to the rapture, was the only way of interpreting what the Bible said. Only recently have non-dispensationalist Evangelicals awakened to the serious dangers that Darbyism poses. Don't take this matter lightly. Challenge those who unwittingly have been led to think and act in accord with ideas of "rapture theology." So much is at stake.

Sincerely,
Tony

9

■ Being Rescued from Fundamentalism

Dear Junia and Timothy,

You are going to find that when you tell people that you are Evangelicals, they will assume that you are Fundamentalists. There's a big difference between the two. While many Fundamentalists would sometimes like to call themselves Evangelicals, most Evangelicals would not appreciate being called Fundamentalists. Be warned: my attempt to differentiate between these two groups makes for a lengthy letter.

Like Evangelicals, Fundamentalists believe that a personal, transforming relationship with the living resurrected Jesus is the means for salvation. Both groups also adhere to all of the doctrines of the Apostles' Creed. However, there are big differences between these two groups. For instance, Fundamentalists usually are appalled by those Evangelicals who do not believe that the Bible must be taken literally.

Fundamentalists' literalistic interpretation of Scripture became very evident back in 1925, during the famous Scopes trial. As you may recall from your history courses, Williams Jennings Bryan, one of America's most famous populist political leaders and a darling of Fundamentalists, led the prosecution of a Tennessee school teacher, John Scopes, who had dared to violate that state's law by teaching his students Charles Darwin's doctrine of evolution. Scopes's defense attorney was Clarence Darrow, one of America's most renowned lawyers.

During the trial, Darrow made a mockery of Bryan's Fundamentalistic, literal interpretation of Scripture—especially of the claim that all of creation took place in just six twenty-four-hour days. I don't think that Fundamentalism ever fully recovered from what happened at the Scopes trial, though some Fundamentalist scientists are still trying to make the case for a six-day creation and want creationism taught in public schools. Most Evangelicals, however, deem the whole debate over evolution superfluous, believing that it doesn't really matter whether or not creation took place in six twenty-four-hour days, or whether each day of creation, as recorded in Genesis, represented an era or stage in the history of evolution.

One of my friends, when confronted by an angry Fundamentalist who wanted to know if she believed that the biblical story of creation was literally true, answered, "Oh! I believe that it is *more* true than that!" What she wanted to communicate was that there are deep theological insights in the Genesis account of creation that are ultimately more important than any literal interpretation of the creation story will allow. This is not to say that my friend does not take the Bible seriously. She strongly believes that the Bible is an infallible guide for faith and practice. In other words, while she does not believe that the Bible is to be treated as a scientific textbook or perfectly accurate historical account, she is certain that the salvation story, which is the crux of its message, is totally reliable, and that its moral teachings should guide the way we live.

Perhaps most bothersome to Evangelicals is the Fundamentalists' commitment to a subculture that is marked by anti-intellectualism and legalism. Fundamentalists, some Evangelicals claim, are often preoccupied by their *don't*s. When I was growing up in a Fundamentalist environment, dancing was a no-no! I did my best to keep my Fundamentalist friends from knowing that I went to my senior prom. Alcoholic beverages were considered "works of the devil," and movies were regarded as "worldly pleasures" that should be avoided.

Back then, we Fundamentalists, like members of any subculture, had our own language. We didn't go out on dates; we had "times of fellowship." We didn't talk; we "shared." We worked overtime to maintain lifestyles that made us different from people in secular society. Over and over again, we were told by our preachers that, in accord with Romans 12:1–2, we must not "conform to this world."

This Fundamentalist way of life did benefit me in some ways. During my chaotic teenage years, it provided a safe structure for my life. The legalisms kept me from destructive behavior and allowed me time to figure out for myself which guidelines I really needed to give order to my life.

Most of my friends who grew up as Fundamentalists look back, as I do, with a certain appreciation for the stabilizing influence that Fundamentalism, with its fixed rules and unquestioned doctrines, provided during a time in our development when it was hard to make sense out of life. What is sad is that far too many Christians never move beyond the legalisms of Fundamentalism. Instead, they become religious elitists who judgmentally frown upon those who are not as "spiritual" as they think themselves to be.

A religion of rules is not to be compared with a religion of love. That is why Jesus said that although John the Baptist, with his religion of judgment on those who broke God's rules, was great in the kingdom of earth, the least in Jesus's kingdom of love and grace was greater than John (Matthew 11:11).

Fundamentalism has a bad reputation these days. It conjures up images of fanatics who bomb abortion clinics, denigrators of Islam, and triumphalists who believe that they have a God-ordained right to impose their own moral values on the rest of America. This is why many Fundamentalists (e.g., Jerry Falwell and Pat Robertson) often try to avoid the label and call themselves Evangelicals. It's bad PR to be labeled a Fundamentalist today. Needless to say, by usurping our name, they have created a great deal of confusion for the general public. This is why many will assume that you two are Fundamentalists the moment you identify yourselves as Evangelicals. And it is why some Evangelicals, especially young people like you, are considering discarding the name and calling themselves "Red-Letter Christians." I'm not sure that this new name will catch on and provide a way for true Evangelicals to distinguish themselves from Fundamentalists, but it's a good name, so I think it's worth a try.

All of this name confusion is very unfortunate because there was once a time when *Fundamentalist* was not a pejorative term. Originally, it referred to those Christians who were committed to doctrines outlined and defended in a set of books titled *The Fundamentals: A Testimony to the Truth*. Back in the early twentieth century, 3 million copies of these books were printed and sent free of charge to Protestant church workers throughout the English-speaking world. If you ever get a chance to review them, you will find them to be an excellent summary by reputable scholars of beliefs that must be upheld if Christianity is to be faithful to its historic origins.

These books were written in opposition to the "modernist theology" coming out of nineteenth-century Germany. Julius Wellhausen and others in German universities had raised serious doubts about the veracity of Scripture. For instance, they claimed that the first five books of the Bible were not really written by Moses under the inspiration of the Holy Spirit, but rather were nothing more than a compilation of writings, often copied from Babylonian literature.

Theologians such as Albrecht Ritschl reduced the New Testament to little more than a guidebook for social and personal ethics. The followers of the then-famous Friedrich Daniel Schleiermacher reduced the Christian experience to subjective mystical feelings that did not require any kind of connectedness with a transcended God. It was in response to such deviations from orthodox Christianity that *The Fundamentals* carefully delineated what could not be compromised to modernism.

The Fundamentals caused a sensation. The books served as a manifesto for those who opposed the German modernists. It is important to note that it was in the context of the ongoing struggle between modernism and Fundamentalism that a dynamic New York preacher, Harry Emerson Fosdick, preached a sermon titled "Shall the Fundamentalists Win?" Thus, he gave a name to those who wanted to defend the "old-time religion."

What concerned Fosdick was not so much the doctrines outlined in *The Fundamentals* as the anti-intellectual tendencies that seemed evident in those who allied themselves with the emergent Fundamentalist movement. He was convinced that if Christianity was to survive in the twentieth century, it had to take seriously the challenges to the faith that were being raised in the academic community. The intellectually sophisticated congregation to which Fosdick preached each Sunday required a Christianity that could be synthesized with the rational and scientific worldview that had become pervasive in the modern world. Any other kind of Christianity, claimed Fosdick, would soon r ender Christianity irrelevant. Fundamentalists, he believed, wanted to freeze theology in forms and definitions that belonged to bygone centuries, leaving little room for the creative reformulations of Christian doctrine essential for what he called "the living of these days."

Fundamentalists were offended by the version of Christianity being propagated by the theological modernists who were making their presence known in most mainline denominations by the beginning of World War I. To them, it seemed as though modernists had extracted ethical and social principles from the Scriptures while discarding much of what did not fit in with a scientific worldview. They viewed the modernists as people who had reduced the Gospel to little more than a manifesto for progressive social reform. For Fundamentalists, to preach anything that sounded like this "social gospel" was to lose what was, in their view, the main purpose of Bible-based preaching: to get people saved from punishment for their sins and ready for Heaven and the bliss of eternal life.

I remember hearing, when I was twelve years old, about the frightening prospect of going to Hell if I failed to decide for Christ. My Fundamentalist preacher seemed to be speaking directly to me as he yelled out, "Are you ready to die?" Even though I was only twelve years old, he scared me—especially when he went on to say, "Even if you don't die, before this week is over, a trumpet could sound, and the Lord could return, and you could be left behind!" Salvation, according to Fundamentalists back then, was only about getting ready for the next world. It had little to do with anything going on in this world.

As the struggles between Fundamentalists and modernists unfolded over the next several decades, Fundamentalists retreated into their own little world. One of their favorite Bible verses was 2 Corinthians 6:17, which reads, "Come ye out from among them and be ye separate"; separate themselves from the rest of the world they did. For entertainment, Fundamentalists often vacationed at the numerous Bible conferences and Christian resorts they had established in locations from coast to coast and watched "Christian films" produced especially for them by their own people. They formed their own colleges and universities, such as Bob Jones University, to keep their young people out of earshot of seductive modernism.

It is fair to say that Fundamentalists became increasingly rigid and close-minded. But lest you become too critical, remember that we are deeply indebted to them for holding on to the essentials of the faith during those days when we lacked the intellectual big guns to fire back in response to modernist attacks on the biblical heritage we hold dear. Early Fundamentalists held the fort, so to speak, until scholarly reinforcements could arrive that would enable us to adequately defend our faith.

Following World War II, things changed for Fundamentalists. Some of them decided that retreat from the dominant culture was no longer necessary. Furthermore, these particular Fundamentalists realized that if they were to fulfill their evangelistic mandate, they would have to discard their isolationism and engage secular society both intellectually and politically. There were progressive social movements afoot, such as the civil-rights movement and the antiwar movement, that demanded a Christian response. Fundamentalists were becoming better educated, with an overwhelming proportion of those who went to institutions of higher education attending secular universities. These students wanted answers to the questions being raised in their classrooms about their faith and practices.

Those Fundamentalists who wanted to engage the outside world on its own turf would come to call themselves "Evangelicals," and it was only a matter of time before they would become a distinct group and establish a separate identity. Junia and Timothy, you are heirs to their efforts.

You need to know of the two men who were especially instrumental in the movement toward worldly engagements: Francis Schaeffer and Carl Henry. The former encouraged us to emerge from our isolation, overcome our sense of inferiority, and begin to engage the skeptics in academia in intelligent dialogue. The latter led us to embrace a progressive social agenda that included ending racism, poverty, and the denigration of women.

Fundamentalists were very slow to follow up on the leads these two men provided. Recently, however, there has been a growing awareness among Fundamentalists that there are solid biblical grounds for what was advocated by Schaeffer and Henry. Unfortunately, it was only a matter of time before an informal schism emerged between progressive Evangelicals and those Fundamentalists who rigidly hold on to separationism and anti-intellectualism.

Francis Schaeffer became an icon for the emerging Evangelical movement. While many of his writings have been negatively critiqued by his recent successors, he demonstrated that scholarly Evangelicals could stand their ground in debates with such modern philosophies as existentialism and positivism. With Schaeffer, Christian apologetics became a renewed possibility.

Since Schaeffer, a host of other Evangelical scholars have emerged. Many of them have doctorate degrees from prestigious universities and can readily defend their convictions and integrate their faith with science and reason in ways that demand respect. Over the years, many of the formerly Fundamentalist Bible colleges and seminaries have evolved into first-rate Evangelical institutions staffed by faculties that can stand tall at any academic gathering. It must be remembered, however, that it was Francis Schaeffer who first helped us to see that escaping from prevailing secular intellectualism was not our only option. It was Schaeffer who showed us that, given a level playing field in the academic world, we could defend ourselves academically and even win some victories.

In 1947, the prominent Evangelical scholar Carl F. H. Henry published a book that has become essential in the history of American Evangelicalism. In *The Uneasy Conscience of Modern Fundamentalism*, Henry made the case that Fundamentalists had overreacted in their opposition to the social Gospel. He criticized Fundamentalists for ignoring biblical imperatives to work for social justice and pointed out that those who neglected the social teachings of Jesus preached only half of the Gospel. A holistic Gospel, he said, not only embraced personal salvation but also required a commitment to work for social justice, especially on behalf of the poor and oppressed. He required Fundamentalists to face the fact that there are almost 2,000 verses of Scripture calling us to serve the poor, and that a host of biblical passages call for faithful Christians to oppose racial discrimination and other forms of social injustice.

Henry's ideas set in motion correctives that eventually helped create the social consciousness of many contemporary Evangelicals. Other writers and preachers, including Ron Sider, the founder of Evangelicals for Social Action, and Jim Wallis, the founder and editor of *Sojourners* magazine, picked up and propagated this message.

Those who refused to budge from preaching a narrow commitment to personal salvation, declining Henry's call for Christians to exercise social responsibility, continued to call themselves Fundamentalists. The rest of us—those who took up Henry's challenge to promote a holistic Gospel—began to call ourselves Evangelicals. We Evangelicals are Christians who, for the most part, accept what was written in *The Fundamentals*. But we argue that faithfulness to the whole Gospel requires commitment to a social-justice agenda.

Many Evangelicals showed signs of dismissing Fundamentalism in cavalier fashion. We assumed that it would gradually fade into oblivion by the turn of the century, and maintain a semblance of life only among backwoods hicks and underclass urbanites. We were very wrong!

Over the last decade and a half, Fundamentalism has made an awesome comeback, and today it is stronger than ever. This resurgence of Fundamentalism has been generated, in no small part, by its leaders' extensive and influential outreach across America through their many radio and television programs. Don't underestimate the importance of this use of electronic media. It is almost impossible these days to spin your dial on the radio without coming across some preacher spouting Darbyite theology and calling listeners to support the Fundamentalist cause. It has been primarily through radio and television that Fundamentalism not only indoctrinates its followers, but also strongly influences Christians in mainline churches. Fundamentalist preachers in radio and television, such as James Dobson, have become household names, and their influence eventually translates into a force to be reckoned with by national political leaders.

The enormous political clout of the Religious Right would not exist today had it not been for Fundamentalist preachers who propagated the conservative political agenda as though it were divinely ordained. Today, most Evangelicals, myself included, feel intimidated by Fundamentalist media personalities because we know that a word of criticism from them can rain down serious trouble on our heads.

As their political power reached into the White House and Congress, Fundamentalists became increasingly triumphalistic. They always talked about "taking over America for Christ" and "making America into a Christian nation," but neither we, nor they themselves, took this rhetoric very seriously. As of late, however, they have become aware that through the power of their media outlets, they can pressure those who have political power into giving them serious attention.

Feminists no longer write them off as "crazies" who want to overturn *Roe v. Wade*. The homosexual community views them as a major threat. Environmentalists consider them as a powerful enemy. Because they have the ability to swing elections their way, their talk about taking over this country and changing its laws to conform to their values is no longer an idle threat. That is why Red-Letter Christians are so important. We are Evangelicals who want to change the world, but *not through political coercion*. Our methodology is loving persuasion. We want Christians to be political but nonpartisan. We don't want power; we just want to speak truth to power. Frankly, we Evangelicals are troubled by the political power that Fundamentalists are wielding these days. Fundamentalist tactics—e.g., efforts to pressure school boards to introduce creationism into classroom curriculums and the distribution in churches of voter guides lauding candidates who espouse Fundamentalist policies—are bound to provoke reactions that will not bode well for anything that has to do with Christianity.

This has been a rather long letter, but there was no shorter way to explain what distinguishes Evangelicals from Fundamentalists, and why, in the days ahead, we just might want to abandon the name Evangelicals and start calling ourselves Red-Letter Christians. It will be painful to change our name, but I'm not sure we have a choice. The label "Evangelical" has picked up a lot of excess baggage over the last few years that I don't want you to have to carry. When Fundamentalists are viewed as rigid legalists committed to an antifeminist, antigay, pro-war agenda, and the secular world associates Evangelicals with Fundamentalists, a new name may be a necessity.

Sincerely,
Tony

10

■ Transcending Partisan Politics

Dear Junia and Timothy,

I really enjoy writing to you because it helps me clarify for myself just who we Evangelicals are. But I think it is also important to give you some idea about who we are *not*.

Given all of the stereotypes surrounding our community, I think it is absolutely vital to explain that Evangelicals are not necessarily Republicans. It may seem like we are, given that in the 2004 elections, more than 80 percent of Evangelicals voted for Republican candidates. Believe it or not, if you don't vote Republican, some fellow Evangelicals will question whether you are a true Christian.

It wasn't always this way. In the nineteenth century, Evangelicals were very often at the vanguard of progressive politics. Remember that the abolitionist John Brown at Harpers Ferry was a fiery Evangelical with a Bible in one hand and a spear in the other. Charles Finney, the dominant evangelist of the nineteenth century, was a major player in the antislavery movement, and his revivals provided much of the impetus for the women's suffrage movement as well. Back in those days, Evangelicals pulled their churches out of mainline denominations not because the denominations were too socially liberal on the race issue, but because they were not liberal enough. In the early twentieth century, William Jennings Bryan, a Fundamentalist icon, was twice the Democratic candidate for the presidency, running as a populist advocate of progressive politics.

Through much of the twentieth century, the Evangelical vote was split evenly between the two major political parties—and in the Southern states, most Evangelicals voted Democrat. As I've explained, many Evangelicals remained largely indifferent to politics, and dismissed theologically liberal Christians for their efforts to change the world through their "social Gospel."

But things started to change as of January 22, 1973, when the Supreme Court handed down the famous *Roe v. Wade* decision, making abortion legal during the first trimester of a woman's pregnancy. Political indifference was no longer an option. Most Evangelicals believed then, as we do now, that an abortion is the killing of an unborn child. After *Roe* was handed down, Evangelicals were convinced that it was our God-required obligation to get involved in politics and elect representatives who would pass pro-life legislation and a president who would appoint pro-life judges.

The strategists of the Republican Party were quick to pick up on our intense pro-life commitments. They recognized that they could sweep Evangelicals into their camp by putting a pro-life plank into their platform and having their candidates speak at pro-life rallies. Personally, I'm not all that convinced that these strategists were as concerned about protecting life as they appeared to be. They very much wanted to reel in the Evangelical vote, but they also wanted to keep on board those "country-club Republicans" who supported the party because of its economic policies, not its moral values. This latter group, represented by the likes of Christine Todd Whitman of New Jersey, tended to be pro-choice, and the party strategists knew it. Consequently, I believe, many Republican law makers decided to keep Evangelicals happy by talking the talk of being pro-life, though they didn't always walk the walk by enacting anti-abortion legislation (which would anger the country-club types).

A number of prominent televangelists helped bring Evangelicals into the Republican fold. In the late 1970s and early 1980s, Jerry Falwell emphasized his pro-life crusade on his TV shows to recruit Christians across the country into his socially conservative organization, the Moral Majority. The success of this movement was far-reaching. After the 1980 election, Falwell rightly declared that the Moral Majority had breathed new life into the Republican Party and played a major role in getting Ronald Reagan elected. In 1988, televangelist Pat Robertson joined the fray against the so-called liberal Democratic establishment and founded another, even more potent, political organization. With the help of field organizer Ralph Reed, Robertson created the Christian Coalition, which went from success to success, eventually playing a major role in sweeping the pro-choice Democratic Congress out of office in 1994.

Over the past decade, yet another Evangelical personality has gained media prominence, becoming the most powerful voice for the so-called family values now embraced by the Republican Party. Of course I'm speaking of James Dobson, who has mobilized tens of millions of Christians to support the Republican political agenda through his *Focus on the Family* radio shows. The significance of his power became evident when the public learned that President George W. Bush had looked to Dobson for approval before nominating a Supreme Court judge.

While these media-savvy Evangelical leaders continue to push for pro-life legislation, they have recently taken an equally vocal stance against homosexual marriage. Believing that gay marriages undermine traditional marriages, they have gone so far as to push for an amendment to the U.S. Constitution that would allow only heterosexual marriages to be recognized as legally valid. Karl Rove, chief political strategist for George W. Bush, ensured Bush's election to a second term as president by putting referendums against gay marriages on the ballots of several key states—including Ohio. It worked! Evangelicals who believed that legalizing gay marriage would be an attack on family values came to the polls in record numbers. This strategy ensured a victory for the politically vulnerable incumbent, George W. Bush, and maintained his party's power in Congress. Consequently, there is little doubt that Evangelicals have become a solid base of support for the Republicans.

Given the very public marriage between Evangelicals and the Republican Party, it is easy to understand why people assume that anyone who identifies as an Evangelical is a Republican with a politically conservative mindset. However, you can rest assured that there is a significant minority of Evangelicals who don't toe the Republican party line. When I am asked whether I'm a Republican or a Democrat, I answer, "Cite the issue." On some issues, I'm in harmony with Republican views; but on other issues, I am more aligned with the positions taken by the Democrats.

I am not alone. A significant number of Evangelicals believe that, as important as issues of gay marriage and abortion may be, there are a host of other issues that also demand our attention. I will be writing about several of these issues—including war, the environment, and the role of women in the church—in subsequent letters. But here I want to address some issues that I consider particularly important and that set us Red-Letter Christians at funda-mental odds with the Religious Right.

Poverty is an absolutely crucial issue, and one that all Evangelicals should care about deeply. More than 2,000 verses of Scripture remind us that responding to the needs of the poor is among the highest obligations of the people of God. In Matthew 25, Jesus declares that there will be a day when the nations will be judged according to how well they cared for needy people. He also said, "Where your treasure is, there will your heart be also" (Matthew 6:21).

Looking at the 2006 federal budget, you would have to conclude that the folks currently in Washington do not have much of a heart for the poor. The fact is that less than four-tenths of 1 percent of the federal budget is designated to help the poor of Third World coun-tries, whereas a full 17 percent is designated for mili-tary spending. I know Americans are concerned with national security, but we have to learn that our security is more dependent on the friends we make than the armies we deploy. We Americans represent 6 percent of the world's population, but we consume 43 percent of the world's resources. To give back to the world's poor such a limited proportion of our government's spend-ing isn't right.

There are many other problems with the way the government spends our money. The federal government has made dramatic reductions in expenditures for medical care and prescription drugs for the poor and the eld-erly, along with draconian cuts in spending on after-school tutoring programs for needy children. At the same time, the new budget provides major tax benefits for the richest people in our society. That's wrong!

Some of our Christian brothers and sisters will say it's not the government's job to use taxpayers' dollars to care for the poor, and that charity is the responsibility of the church. They will readily agree that Jesus has called his followers to minister to the needs of the poor, but then go on to claim that there's nothing in Scripture that requires governments to assume that responsibility. I have to respond to their argument by quoting what Bono, an internationally known rock star and spokesman for the poor, said at the 2006 National Prayer Breakfast: "It's not about charity. It's about justice."

For the most part, the church has done brilliantly when it comes to charity. Whenever there's a catastro-phe (for instance, Hurricane Katrina), church folks, and especially Evangelicals, show up to volunteer their help by the tens of thousands, and they shell out dollars by the millions. But I believe the church also has a responsi-bility to call upon the government to do justice. One Old Testament prophet said that the Lord requires us "to do justice, to love mercy, and to walk humbly with our God" (Micah 6:8). The prophet Isaiah makes it clear that those in government will be held responsible for what happens to "poor widows and orphans" (Isaiah

10:1–2). A government that serves the interests of the rich to the neglect of the poor is not doing justice.

One of the major reasons that politically progressive people like us seem dangerous to Evangelicals on the Religious Right is that we question laissez-faire capitalism. This is heresy to people who believe that capitalism is somehow ordained by God.

Now, don't get me wrong—we very much affirm the free-enterprise system. We affirm free enterprise because we are convinced that we as individuals, and not the state, should make decisions about our lives. God gave such freedom to Adam and Eve in Eden, and we believe that this same freedom to choose what we would do and be is what God wants for us. That is free enterprise.

But while we believe in free enterprise, we reject the "greed principle" that motivates so many in the capitalistic world. Capitalism relies on the idea that people work solely for profits. By contrast, we believe that Christians should be motivated by love to serve God by meeting the needs of others (2 Corinthians 5:14).

In a consumer-oriented capitalistic economic system, a great deal of what is produced doesn't meet anybody's needs, but is simply designed to generate profits. People do not need cigarettes or oversized hamburgers. There is no need for hunters to have machine guns that fire a hundred rounds of bullets in minutes. Nor is there a need for gas-guzzling SUVs. Producing a vast array of consumer goods that nobody needs wastes the limited, non-renewable resources of our world. And while we squander such resources to satisfy our artificially created wants, the basic needs of a billion people in the Third World go unmet.

As countercultural as this may seem, we progressive Evangelicals advocate a simple lifestyle. We say it is immoral to be sucked into the affluent spending habits promoted by the marketing techniques of commercialistic capitalism. We call our fellow Christians to live simply, so that the poor of the world might simply live.

Capitalism has created huge corporations that make gigantic profits by exploiting cheap labor in poor countries. The Bible specifically addresses this kind of injustice in James 5:1–4:

> *Go to now, ye rich men, weep and howl for your miseries that shall come upon you. Your riches are corrupted, and your garments are moth-eaten. Your gold and silver is cankered; and the rust of them shall be a witness against you, and shall eat your flesh as if it were fire. Ye have heaped treasure together for the last days. Behold, the hire of the laborers who have reaped down your fields, which is of you kept back by fraud, crieth: and the cries of them which have reaped are entered into the ears of the Lord of Sabaoth.*

But exploitive big-time capitalists aren't the only problem. We are all complicit in the injustice of world poverty. Remember that the bargain prices that you and I pay at supermarkets and malls exist because people in other countries have been underpaid for their labor. Such realities are endemic to the capitalistic system, and it is this system that we critique with biblical principles.

None of what I have said about capitalism is meant to keep you out of the business world. In fact, I am hoping for just the opposite. I pray that young people like you two will seriously consider vocations in the American free-enterprise system and demonstrate how companies can make profits while producing good things that meet people's needs; paying workers a fair share of these profits; and seeing to it that industrial production does not harm the environment. That's a tall order, but the Bible says that from those to whom much is given, much is expected (Luke 12:48).

At Eastern University, where I have taught for many years, an MBA program has been created that demonstrates how the free-enterprise system can be used to further the mission of the church. In this program, we train Christians to be entrepreneurs in Third World countries. We are creating a new kind of missionary who is trained in what it takes to start small businesses and cottage industries in the slums and barrios where the unemployed poor live. These missionaries help alleviate economic poverty in the best possible way. By creating jobs for the poor, we offer them an escape from poverty while leaving their dignity in tact. We share with our students these words of Lao Tzu:

> Go to the people, live among them.
> Learn from them, plan with them.
> Build on what they have.
> Teach by showing, learn by doing.
> Not relief but release,
> and when the task is finished
> and when their work is done,
> the people will remark,
> "We have done it ourselves."

A free-enterprise system built on values like that can be a means for economic salvation. Capitalism is here to stay. It is the most efficient system imaginable for producing consumer goods at the lowest possible price. Even the leaders of the People's Republic of China understand that. Your mission is to work to maximize the good that it can do, and to see to it that it does justice to the poor.

I really considered whether or not it was a good idea to take up so much of your time explaining what we progressive Evangelicals are *not*, but then I remembered a quote from the writings of that Danish philosopher/ theologian, Søren Kierkegaard: "One can only be a Christian in contrast and contrastedly."

I don't know where you will come down on the issues that I have discussed here and will discuss in the letters that follow. But I hope you will understand that being Evangelical requires that you think for yourself. In the words of Scripture, you are to "work out your own salvation with fear and trembling" (Philippians 2:12). I hope you will never let yourselves get into an intellectual lock-step with others so that you end up uncritically buying into a prescribed theology and a partisan political agenda. You must learn to think critically when preachers and teachers spell out for you what you should believe.

I myself claim no special handle on truth, and what I tell you will require serious critiquing on your part. Some beliefs about Christ and the salvation story are rock-solid foundations for us Evangelicals; but thinking for yourselves about everything else is in harmony with the Evangelical tradition. When you enter an Evangelical household, you are not expected to leave your brains at the door.

Sincerely,
Tony

11

■ Abortion as a Defining Issue

Dear Junia and Timothy,

As you venture forth to live out your Evangelical commitments, two issues will haunt you at every turn: abortion and homosexuality. These two issues are presently causing widespread controversies throughout Christendom. To say that Evangelicals are hung up on these two subjects is an understatement. They've become the defining issues of our times. Anyone who is pro-choice or in favor of gay marriage can expect to be persona non grata in most Evangelical circles. These are emotional hot buttons, and they are rarely discussed thoughtfully. As you face up to these two issues, it is critical that you know what you're talking about.

I'm not going to tell you what to think about either issue, but because Evangelicals often are characterized as monolithic on both issues, I think it's important for you to understand that there's a much broader variety of opinion within our community than you might think. I'll begin with abortion.

Let's start with the obvious: Evangelicals are overwhelmingly pro-life. While the Bible itself does not specifically address abortion, many theologians, from the time of St. Augustine through the present day, have argued that at the moment of conception, the unborn zygote is "ensouled." Many Christians, including most Evangelicals, believe that something miraculous occurs at the instant of conception: the zygote is transformed from an assemblage of organic cells in the mother's womb into a human being. The embryo becomes a sacred creation, bearing the image of God. Believing in these principles, most Evangelicals argue that destruction of the unborn embryo is murder, but there is no way to prove that they are right. This doctrine leaves many questions unanswered such as those posed by Francis Collins, the famous geneticist, who was in charge of the government's genome project. In response to the Augustinian theology, that there is an ensoulment at the moment of conception, Collins points out that it is not until after conception that the zygote that generates twins is separated into two separate entities. Therefore, he asks, "Are there two souls infused in the single zygote at conception? Does one of the twins end up deprived of a soul? Or do the twins have to share a soul?" As you can see the abortion issue may not be as easy to address as most Evangelicals tend to assume. Nevertheless, among Evangelicals, there is an unshaken general consensus that Augustine was right.

Given this conviction, and the fact that there are approximately a million abortions performed in America each year, it's not surprising that Evangelical preachers at pulpits across the country regularly compare the practice of abortion in America to the Holocaust. It is no wonder that these same preachers tell their congregations that Evangelical Christians should not support any political party or candidate for public office that is pro-choice (i.e., the Democratic Party). So emphatic are our Evangelical spokespersons on this issue that they, along with most of their followers, often become single-issue candidates at election time. No matter how much they might agree with the positions of a candidate on all of the other issues on the table, if that candidate is pro-choice, most Evangelicals are likely to vote against him or her, and to urge all other Christians to do the same.

Nonetheless, there is an ongoing discussion among Evangelicals about the issue of abortion and how we should address it. For instance, some of our people believe that while abortion is wrong, making it illegal will do little to solve the problem. Outlawing abortions, they say, will only drive abortions underground. Then, they argue, abortions will be performed in back alleys by butchers, or with coat hangers by pregnant women themselves. Furthermore, they point out that the statistics available for abortions in 1950, before *Roe v. Wade* legalized abortion, indicate that the number of abortions was astoundingly high. Those statistics are often cited as evidence that making abortions illegal will not deter those who are desperate.

Many Evangelicals believe that we should be working instead to make abortions rare while keeping them legal. They offer concrete proposals for programs that would help women who may consider abortion for economic reasons. For instance, they advocate government-funded medical coverage for pregnant women, too many of whom can't afford doctors and hospital care. Likewise, they advocate daycare programs so that mothers can be gainfully employed and thus able to support themselves and their children. They support proposals for raising the minimum wage so that unmarried mothers can earn a decent living and support their children. (Studies show that a person working full-time at minimum wage cannot even pay rent on a typical apartment.) Other ideas include laws providing guaranteed maternity leaves so that women don't have to choose between job security and motherhood, and special programs to allow young mothers to stay in school and complete their education. Without at least a high-school education, most unwed mothers are doomed to poverty. Finally, Evangelicals themselves can do more to help women who are inclined to have an abortion: they can put themselves forward as adoptive parents. If Evangelicals are so supportive of pro-life legislation, then they should be willing to adopt the children born from unwanted pregnancies. Presently, thousands of children are left in foster care because no one is willing to take them in.

Finally, many of us hold the controversial belief that sex education and contraception should be more widely available. This idea is controversial because many Evangelicals argue that to make such things available is to give tacit approval to sexual intercourse outside of marriage. A recent study by the Guttmacher Institute shows that if Medicaid coverage was to include contraception for low-income women, 200,000 abortions of unwanted pregnancies could be prevented. And if the other measures suggested above were also implemented, I believe the number of abortions performed in America each year could be cut in half. The Religious Right seems to ignore that those conservative candidates that they support each election year regularly vote against such proposals.

Barney Frank, a Democratic congressman from Massachusetts, justifiably mocks Evangelicals by claiming that we believe life "begins at conception and ends at birth." He contends that those same pro-life Evangelicals who argue so strongly against abortion want nothing to do with assuming fiscal responsibility for children born from unwanted pregnancies. As a gay man and a strong voice on many justice issues, Frank is particularly upset that most Evangelicals also want to prohibit gay and lesbian couples from adopting the unwanted babies whom we don't want aborted.

I can understand why many of those who agree with Barney Frank say that we Evangelicals are really not thinking clearly. We want to require women with unwanted pregnancies to give birth, but then we fail to step forward when volunteers are required for adoptions. Aren't we being unfair? More hypocritical still is the fact that an estimated 15 percent of pro-life Evangelical women have had abortions themselves yet favor policies that would deny abortions to women whose social and economic circumstances are often much more difficult.

For most Evangelicals, the struggle over abortion comes down to one question: Is an unborn fetus a human being? If the answer is "yes," then abortion is murder. For most of us, that settles the question. But is opposing abortion all there is to being pro-life? A host of Roman Catholic theologians have come out in support of what Cardinal Joseph Bernardin, the onetime archbishop of Chicago, called the seamless-garment theory. Those who hold to this doctrine believe that we need a "comprehensive and consistent ethic of life" in which opposition to abortion is joined by opposition to war, capital punishment, and euthanasia. If killing is wrong, they argue, then Christians should oppose all forms of killing. Many of our Evangelical leaders—including Jim Wallis of *Sojourners* magazine and Ron Sider of Evangelicals for Social Action—agree with this seamless-garment doctrine, claiming that pro-life advocates who do not oppose all forms of killing are being inconsistent if not hypocritical.

Some Evangelicals *are* pro-choice and support the right of women to have abortions—specifically when the potential consequences of pregnancy and childbirth are dire. Some have even adopted an ideological justification for abortion, making a case that abortion is not murder if performed in the earliest weeks of a pregnancy. They contend that what makes Homo sapiens human is interaction with one or more other humans. The traits that differentiate humans from other animals—language, self-awareness, conscience, and even a sense of the sacred—are all traits that are imparted to a developing person though socialization. The Bible, these pro-choice Evangelicals contend, does not support the Augustinian belief that ensoulment occurs at the moment of conception. Ironically, they use the same passage from Scripture, Isaiah 49:1, often cited by pro-lifers in making their case. That verse reads

The Lord hath called me from the womb;
from the bowels of my mother hath he made
mention of my name.

Pro-life Evangelicals quote this verse to support their argument that there is a sacred humanness to the unborn. This verse, they claim, makes it clear that even the unborn fetus possesses the image of God.

Pro-choice advocates interpret this same verse as a statement that it is not at the instant of conception but *during* the months of uterine development that the embryonic child becomes transformed into a human being. They believe that the mother interacts with the unborn fetus in utero, and that this interaction is what makes the unborn human. But, they argue, this interaction begins not at conception but rather eight or nine weeks later. Until that time, they believe, the fetus lacks a central nervous system connected to an active brain, and hence is incapable of registering or receiving those prenatal social-psychological-spiritual influences that might be forthcoming from the mother and that have the potential of humanizing the unborn child.

Personally, I don't accept this theory. It seems to me like a very convoluted way of explaining what makes an unborn fetus human. More importantly, there is no way of proving it. At best, this explanation may be a good guess as to when and how humanness begins, but it is still only a guess. There is a good possibility of error in this kind of thinking, and I am convinced that it is best to play it safe and side with life. If we don't know for sure when human life begins, ought we not to oppose abortion on the grounds that it *may* result in destroying a human life? I think that the answer to that question should be "Yes!"

While I remain firmly pro-life, however, I should say that a number of things continue to trouble me about my position. One major concern is that it sets me at odds with many of my feminist friends. They believe that I am ignoring the rights of women to control their own bodies. Being able to make decisions that determine our own destinies is the essence of human freedom, and my Christian feminist friends argue strongly that anti-abortion laws take away that freedom. To this, many pro-life advocates respond, "But what about the rights of the unborn? Shouldn't their right to life be protected?"

It is my job, and the job of Evangelical males more generally, to convince people that when we stand behind pro-life legislation, we do so out of a deeply felt religious faith and not because we simply want to control women. It would help considerably if we didn't continually have austere men serving as the spokespersons for our position. When there is a public pronouncement against abortion, that pronouncement is most often made by a man, with a predominance of other men standing in the background. It just doesn't sit well with me when a man represents the pro-life position in TV debates on abortion. You probably have the same kind of negative reactions I do in response to that kind of thing. Pro-life Evangelicals should make sure that women are their spokespersons. It might help challenge the argument that the pro-life stance is simply a male-dominance thing.

What troubles me most about the continuing debate on abortion is that there seems to be no middle ground. The issue is intensely polarizing, and I think that is the way many people on both sides want it to be. Pro-life advocates say that if the unborn is a human being, en-souled by God and created in the image of God, then there can be no compromise with pro-choice people. Likewise, pro-choice advocates argue that a woman has the fundamental right to make decisions about her own body and that, in a society that claims a wall of separation between church and state, there can be no yielding of legal rights to what they consider to be the beliefs of religious Fundamentalists.

And yet, in spite of this polarized rhetoric, most Americans hold more moderate positions—as do most Evangelicals. Some studies indicate that up to 70 percent of us Evangelicals take positions between the two extremes. On the one hand, there is a consensus, even among the general public, that life is sacred and should not be destroyed in a seemingly arbitrary manner (which is what happens when abortion is reduced to a form of birth control for the sexually promiscuous). On the other hand, there is great sympathy for the 25,000 women who become pregnant each year because of rape, and especially for the countless girls who are impregnated because of incest.

Those who take a more moderate stance are deeply troubled by the belief held by many intensely pro-life advocates, and especially many Roman Catholic theologians, that the life of the unborn must be preserved even when the mother's life is endangered. The willingness to allow the death of a mother in order to preserve the life of a not-yet-born child is unacceptable to most people, including most Evangelicals. Consequently, there are many, many people who, like former president Jimmy Carter, claim to be pro-life but opposed to making abortion illegal.

There is another reason that we should be careful about slipping into the kind of polarizing rhetoric that all too often characterizes the abortion debate. Studies have shown that when states have passed laws forbidding all abortions, regardless of circumstances, a reaction takes place in which many people come to favor the pro-choice position. In demanding complete capitulation to their point of view, the pro-life advocates in the Evangelical community might just end up losing the battle to save the unborn.

This issue is not going to go away, because there is no way to prove whether or not an unborn fetus is a human being in the image of God. Abortion will continue to be one of the hot potatoes that we Evangelicals find difficult to handle. In the end, it is our faith commitments that establish the positions that we take. But as you formulate your own thinking on this issue, remember that there are good people on both sides of the argument. The name calling that labels pro-life people as "nazis" and pro-choice people as "murderers" does nothing but increase animosity and retard any loving rapprochement between the two warring sides.

Recently, one of the leaders of the pro-life movement had a series of private face-to-face discussions with a prominent spokesperson for the pro-choice side. They discovered in each other a sincerity and goodness that enabled them to be friends in spite of their serious differences. Maybe they could teach the rest of us something about how those on opposite sides of a crucial argument should treat each other. Remember, God has called us to a ministry of reconciliation (2 Corinthians 5:18).

Sincerely,
Tony

12

■ Being Straight but Not Narrow

Dear Junia and Timothy,

Gay marriage has become an issue almost as divisive as abortion within the Evangelical community. Let me be up front with you and tell you that I'm a conservative on this issue. While I stand steadfastly with my gay and lesbian friends as they struggle for equality and justice, I personally think that same-sex marriage runs contrary to what the apostle Paul sets forth in the first chapter of Romans, verses 23–27:

> *. . . exchanging the glory of the immortal God for an image shaped like mortal man, even for images like birds, beasts and reptiles. For this reason God has given them up to their own vile desires and the consequent degradation of their bodies . . . women have exchanged natural intercourse for unnatural, and men too, giving up natural relations with women, burn with lust for one another; males behave*

indecently with males, and are paid in their own
persons the fitting wage of such perversion.

Furthermore, I believe that there has been a unified understanding throughout the church's 2,000-year history that these verses should be interpreted as a prohibition on same-sex eroticism. These verses seem clear to me, and the way they have been interpreted by church tradition over the years settles the case for me.

Not all Evangelical Christians, however, agree with me or with church tradition when it comes to gay marriage. My wife, Peggy, opposes my conservative point of view. She reads the same passage from Romans as a tirade against idolatry. She believes that what Paul was really condemning in this passage were the abominable sexual practices often connected with idolatrous worship. Peggy points out that Paul was in the city of Corinth when he wrote these words, and that the prevailing religion of that city included homosexual orgies as part of its idolatrous worship. The deity that was worshipped in Corinth was Aphrodite, and in the worship of Aphrodite, all men, heterosexual as well as homosexual, were required to engage in same-sex erotic activities, and women were required to do the same with other women. Peggy claims that a fair reading of Romans 1:23–27 will show that Paul was condemning the licentious practices that went on in pagan temples, not the loving commitment of same-sex couples.

It wouldn't take much for me to buy into Peggy's argument, except that it flies in the face of how saints through the ages have understood this passage. I think it might be a bit arrogant for her to say, "I'm right, and 2,000 years of church tradition are wrong." Peggy responds to that accusation by pointing out that church tradition has been wrong before, such as in its handling of slavery and the role of women. And yet, despite all of Peggy's arguments, I continue to hold a more conservative interpretation of these verses from Romans. I believe that my stance is backed by church tradition.

I tend to focus my attention on this Romans passage because I think it is the clearest and most important biblical passage that addresses the issue of homosexuality. Other passages allude to homosexual practices, but they are less clear. One verse that is sometimes mentioned is 1 Timothy 1:9–10. Here, Paul attacks a very specific form of sexual perversion called pederasty, in which boys were castrated before puberty to keep them "soft" (devoid of the traits of mature males), thus making them more desirable for predators. This hardly can be equated with committed relationships of same-sex couples.

Another passage in the New Testament that is often referenced in discussions on homosexuality is 1 Corinthians 6:9. This passage, however, is somewhat problematic. Some translators contend that it is a clear condemnation of erotic homosexual behavior, but there is sufficient evidence that these translators might be a bit presumptuous. The Greek word *arsenokoite*, which some translators believe refers to homosexuals, is really quite ambiguous. Since it is difficult to discover the meaning of that word from other literature of the time, most Bible scholars say that we can be certain only that the word refers to some kind of sexual perversion.

There are passages in the Old Testament that deal with homosexual behavior, but my wife and Christians like her believe that such passages are of minimal significance. They contend that, in order to properly weigh the importance of these verses, we must understand that there are two kinds of rules in the Hebrew Bible—purity codes and moral laws. The purity codes are basically what we would call kosher rules. For instance, Orthodox Jews who obey these laws will not eat ham or shellfish. These purity laws, say most scholars, must be distinguished from the moral codes (i.e., the Ten Commandments).

Those who seek to legitimate gay marriage argue that the condemnations of homosexual eroticism in the books of Leviticus and Deuteronomy are part of the purity codes, and should no longer be understood as binding on Christians. This, they say, is because Jesus transcended the purity codes, and Peter's dream recorded in Acts 10:9–15 illustrated that the purity codes were not to be observed by the Christian community. They point out that the passage in the Old Testament that refers to homosexual erotic behavior as "an abomination" comes right after a passage that describes touching the skin of a dead pig as an abomination in the eyes of God—which puts the Super Bowl into serious question!

Nevertheless, I am troubled by the cavalier manner in which some who are allied with my wife seem to dismiss such passages. It's worth noting that most Jewish rabbis believe that the seriousness of any law in the Torah should be understood in the context of the punishment to be meted out when that law is violated. To commit a homosexual act, according to the laws of Moses, was punishable by death. That makes a strong case for taking the rulings against homosexual eroticism in the Hebrew Bible quite seriously. To this argument, Peggy responds by asking, "You are not suggesting that we take that prescribed punishment seriously and start putting gays to death, are you?" When I answer, "Of course not!" she smiles and asks, "Well if you take those rules from the Hebrew Bible so seriously, then why not?"

If you are going to be Red-Letter Christians, it is important for you to recognize that there is no record in the New Testament of Jesus saying anything about homosexuality, but he is quite specific about condemning divorce and the remarriage of divorced persons. Peggy would ask, "Don't you think it's hypocritical for Evangelicals like you to accept into the church, and even ordain to the ministry, persons who have been divorced and remarried, but to turn around and forbid gay marriage?" She goes on to ask, "How can you accept marriages that Jesus specifically condemns, and then turn around and oppose marriages Jesus never even mentions?" My only response is that the prohibitions against homosexual eroticism were so prevalent in his time that Jesus saw no need to talk about the obvious. But my wife doesn't buy that argument.

Gay marriage is a hot-button issue these days. Political strategists such as Karl Rove know how to push this button, confident that a host of Evangelicals will go ballistic with upset and turn out on Election Day to vote their outrage. Opposition to gay marriage has been responsible for determining elections both locally and nationally. We have let political strategists turn gay marriage into the most divisive issue in Christendom. Conservatives believe that legalizing gay marriage will undermine traditional marriage and contribute to bringing down this already shaky institution.

I think Evangelicals spend far too much time worrying about gay marriage. Conservative Evangelicals would have you believe that gay and lesbian civil unions would weaken the institution of marriage. I think that's absurd! It's true that the institution of marriage is in serious jeopardy these days, but that's not because there are gays and lesbians who want their unions recognized. The reality is that divorce is destroying the American family. It's heterosexuals who are getting divorced; gays want to be married!

In fact, my wife and others have argued that gays and lesbians are actually lending support to the institution of marriage in seeking to be married. These couples are declaring that they are rejecting promiscuity and want to affirm the lifelong loving commitment that exemplifies marriage at its best. I fail to see how such lifelong commitments by gays hurt the rest of us. Instead, they send a message that commitments for life can provide one of life's most humanizing relationships. Even if you don't agree, I hope you can understand how one could contend that both civil unions and same-sex marriages could actually strengthen the institution of marriage.

However I might disagree with Peggy over the issue of gay marriage, I think it is essential to point out that, in spite of all the attention the subject gets these days among our Evangelical brothers and sisters, homosexuality is not the dominant concern of Scripture. Neither side of this controversy has overwhelming and inarguable support from Scripture for its position, although each side thinks it does. And yet Evangelicals have made this a defining issue and are ready to foster schisms in the churches over it. While I want to stress that whether or not to accept homosexual marriage is an important concern that requires ongoing discussion within Christendom, it shouldn't cause divisions among us. My marriage shows that it is possible to have a serious difference of opinion on this issue without getting a divorce. Therefore, I don't see why churches should split up over it.

Although I maintain a conservative interpretation of Scripture when dealing with this issue, I differ from many Evangelicals in believing that people do not choose to be gay and that changes in sexual orientation are unlikely. I am sad to say that some of our most famous radio preachers and televangelists have led a large segment of the Evangelical community to accept the erroneous belief that homosexuality is a malady that can be cured with prayer and proper counseling. They condemn any suggestion that genetic or other biophysical factors might underlie homosexual orientation. Speaking with an air of certainty—which almost all social scientists will tell you is unsubstantiated—these preachers claim not only to know what causes the homosexual orientation, but also how to counteract those causes and turn gays and lesbians into heterosexuals.

These pseudo-experts generally explain homosexual orientation by way of a worn-out neo-Freudian theory. According to this theory, homosexuality results from a faulty identification the child makes with the opposite-sex parent during the early phases of socialization. You will often hear radio preachers explaining that, if a boy has a weak and ineffectual father and a strong, dominant mother, the boy will identify with his mother rather than his father and become gay. These pseudo-experts urge fathers to play rough-and-tumble games with their sons and to make sure that every boy knows that "the man is the head of the house."

If this theory were true, then the African American male population would be disproportionately gay. This is because, when compared to the rest of U.S. society, there are a disproportionate number of homes in the African American community with no adult male presence. Yet there is absolutely no evidence that homosexuality is disproportionately prevalent among African American men. Such empirical evidence, however, has never hindered these preachers from making their bold assertions.

This theory of the weak or absent father is only one of many ways in which Evangelicals and many others try to convince people that upbringing rather than nature determines sexual orientation. Of course, this notion carries with it the idea that it's possible to "undo" homosexuality. This idea is what upsets me most about such theories. It inflicts incredible damage not only on gays and lesbians but also on their parents.

Just stop and consider the sorrow parents might experience upon finding out that a son or daughter is homosexual. These parents know that their child will grow up in a world filled with prejudice against gays and lesbians. They will undoubtedly weep knowing that, given the nature of society, their child is likely to endure much suffering, including deep feelings of alienation and, in many cases, self-hatred. The last thing these troubled parents need is some know-it-all preacher pointing a finger at them and saying, "It's all your fault."

To lay false guilt trips on hurting parents is a horrible thing to do. As if that were not bad enough, most of these same preachers tell parents that their children could be "cured" if they really wanted to be, and that it's only the rebellious attitudes of their children that keep them from taking the steps that will change them into heterosexuals. I have gotten reports that some Evangelical leaders urge parents to ostracize children who refuse to seek change, believing that such "tough love" might drive these children to repent of their rebellion against a cure and get the spiritual help needed for deliverance. The painful testimonies I hear from sons and daughters who have been cut off from their parents because of such advice makes my blood boil.

The idea that homosexuality is a curable condition is incredibly destructive for parents, but it is all the more so for gay men and women themselves. This idea creates unrealistic expectations and tremendous pain for homosexuals who want to change their orientations. Some homosexuals have been driven to despair, and even suicide, after the therapies that were supposed to "fix" them failed. I am not suggesting that there's never been a single instance wherein a person's sexual orientation really has been changed. But I am saying that holding up a high probability of change is offering false hope and causing further emotional and spiritual pain for a host of people who are already suffering. I have had scores of gays tell me how they have paced the floor all night in prayer, begging God to change them, with no results. Over and over, I've had to listen to young people who have spent a fortune on Christian psychologists offering hope for a cure, all to no avail.

There are a handful of Christians out there who do claim to have changed sexual orientation, but they are very few in number. I suspect that most of them were really bisexuals who only changed from one sexual behavioral pattern to another. Nevertheless, I believe that God can do anything, so I will never say "never." But I don't expect many miracles when it comes to changing sexual orientation. Accuse me of being a man of little faith, but that's what I think the evidence supports.

Currently, a great many Evangelical leaders are leading crusades aimed at denying gay and lesbian couples many of the basic civil rights that the rest of us enjoy.

If these leaders have their way, gay couples who have made lifelong commitments to each other will be denied a variety of benefits that committed heterosexual couples enjoy. In fact, the U.S. Government Accountability Office cites 1,138 rights that heterosexual couples enjoy that are presently denied homosexual couples. A small sample of these injustices includes the denial of Social Security benefits to gay couples; the refusal of auto-insurance companies in some states to cover same-sex partners; prohibitions against gay couples' joint ownership of homes and businesses; denials of food stamps and low-cost housing for poor gay couples; the denial of veterans' benefits for the partners of gay veterans; denials in many states and hospitals of same-sex partners' access to medical records and visitation rights; and, in many states, the option of courts to set aside the will of a homosexual so that her or his partner does not receive the intended inheritance.

The list could go on and on.

When asked whether I believe that state governments should legalize gay and lesbian marriages, I respond in a way that might provide some satisfaction to people on both sides of the debate. *I propose that the government should get out of the marrying business completely.* Instead, the state should legally recognize and grant the same legal benefits to both heterosexual and homosexual unions. But the state should not call these unions "marriages" because, I believe, marriage is religiously ordained and belongs solely in the hands of religious institutions. Marriage, I believe, has been instituted by God, and the government should have nothing to do with it. When I perform wedding ceremonies, I find it incongruous that, after reading Scripture, praying, and explaining what marriage is all about in the eyes of God, I am required to end by saying, "And now, by the authority given unto me by the state of Pennsylvania, I now pronounce you man and wife."

"Wait a minute!" I say to myself. "When did I cease serving under the authority of God and become a civil servant? Isn't there confusion between church and state in these roles? Isn't what the state does separate from the spiritual significance that the church gives to the relationship?" I want to separate the two functions to end this confusion.

I believe that we should initiate the system employed in the Netherlands, wherein two people who want to make a lifetime commitment to each other go down to City Hall and register as a legally recognized couple so that they can receive all the rights and privileges available to such couples. Then, if that couple is religious, they should go to a church, synagogue, or mosque and have their union blessed.

This scheme of separating civil unions from marriages is increasingly operative across Europe. Those who don't believe in gay marriage would get married in churches that support their convictions. On the other hand, gay couples could seek out churches that would bless their civil unions and make these unions into marriages. The different churches that my wife and I belong to illustrate how this might work. I belong to a church congregation that believes that gay marriage is unacceptable. My wife, who differs with me on this issue, belongs to a church that "blesses and celebrates" gay marriage. No compromises in beliefs or practices are necessary for either of us or our congregations—and that's the way it should be.

Don't lose sight of the fact that many of our Evangelical brothers and sisters are trying to deny homosexuals rights other than marriage. For instance, some want to deny gays and lesbians the opportunity to teach in public schools, even though there is no evidence that they would prove any more dangerous to students than heterosexual teachers. There is a destructive myth suggesting that homosexuals are inevitably predators on children. This, of course, is just that—a myth. True, cases can be cited in which gays and lesbians have hit on students sexually, but I suspect that the likelihood of this happening is the same per capita for heterosexuals. Given how many more heterosexuals than homosexuals teach in our schools, it is obvious where the greatest danger lies. There is no question in my mind that those who prey on children are especially reprehensible. Jesus said that "whosoever shall offend one of these little ones that believe in me, it is better for him that a millstone were hanged about his neck, and he were cast into the sea" (Mark 9:42). But to denigrate homosexuals by claiming that they are especially dangerous to children is to ignore the facts. What I find further disturbing is that such claims form the basis for the often-successful attempts by Evangelical leaders to prevent gay and lesbian couples from adopting children.

Scientific studies have shown that children raised by homosexual couples are no more inclined to adopt a homosexual lifestyle than are children in the general population. Nevertheless, some Evangelicals fight actively to prevent children without families from being adopted by caring gay couples who would give them safe and loving environments. Certain gay couples are eager to adopt even HIV-positive children, many of whom would not otherwise be adopted. Still, many Evangelicals balk at the idea of gay adoptions, even in these cases. If anybody ought to shudder at the warning of Jesus, it's those who are working overtime to make sure that these motherless and fatherless children never find a loving home. I don't see most of the Evangelicals who oppose gay adoptions stepping forward to take in the many, many children whom no one else wants to adopt.

Some Evangelicals advocate homophobic policies on other issues as well, including the right of gays and lesbians to serve in the armed forces or other government agencies. These Evangelicals fail to remember that this country was started by revolutionaries who claimed that there should be no taxation without representation. On that basis, if gays and lesbians are barred from representation in the military or government agencies, they also should be free from having to pay taxes. If such a provision ever became law, we'd see the biggest coming-out party in history.

Wherever you come out on the controversies that surround homosexuality and gay marriage, I urge you to work for justice for gay and lesbian people. There is no question that the Bible has a whole lot to say about justice for the oppressed. Even those who hold to conservative views will generally agree that homosexuals have to endure injustices and humiliations. Keep the discussion going on these matters, and don't settle for the knee-jerk conclusions too often expressed by our Evangelical sisters and brothers when discussing matters related to homosexuality. For now, let me only reiterate the words of Paul: "Think on these things."

Sincerely,
Tony

13

Loving Muslims in a
Fear-Filled World

Dear Junia and Timothy,

In the coming years, you are going to have to deal with Muslims and the Islamic world. Given the ongoing war on terrorism, it is often difficult to know just what to do and think. On the one hand, you must know that most Muslims are good, peace-loving people who are just as upset by terrorism as are the rest of us. But that doesn't curtail our growing fear of Muslim people. The horrendous actions of a few have created problems for the many.

If you're honest, you probably will admit that it makes you a bit uneasy when men who appear to be from the Middle East get on a plane or bump into you in a shopping center. And you probably hesitate in greeting women in Islamic garb with common courtesies such as a smile or a friendly nod.

Unfortunately, some of our leading Evangelical preachers are inflaming fear by spreading distorted messages about Muhammad and Islam over the airwaves. A former president of America's largest Protestant denomination declared that the Prophet Muhammad, the founder of Islam, was a pedophile. And one of America's leading evangelists has called Islam an "evil religion." Over and over again, radio preachers have gone out of their way to cite verses out of the Koran that they say justify the killing of "infidels" (i.e., non-Muslims). They forget that in our own Bible, our God orders the Jews to practice genocide when Joshua leads the children of Israel on a conquering rampage. We Red-Letter Christians may know that we should discount such accusations against Muslims, but I assure you, they are playing well in the heartland and intensifying fear of Muslims.

In this context, it is hardly surprising that prejudices toward Muslims are growing, even among those who consider themselves open-minded and accepting of cultural diversity. Many of my socially liberal Christian friends support racial profiling of Arabs at airports, even if it means that they will be subjected to humiliating body searches. Just a few years ago, these same "nondiscriminating" and "non-prejudicial" persons would have been outraged at the mere suggestion of such profiling. Some African Americans, who condemned profiling when they were its victims, now think that it may be a necessary evil. Likewise, objections to the monitoring of phone calls by government agents quickly faded when the president assured the public that the government

was *only* monitoring phone calls to "certain countries"—
and we all knew which countries were on his list.

I remember, as a boy, being appalled at reports that
in the Soviet Union there were government spies in
churches on Sunday mornings, checking to see if anything subversive to the state was being spoken from the
pulpit. And yet I was not shocked to learn that our government agents are regularly spying in mosques. I know
that some radical imams are mouthing the kind of in-
flammatory rhetoric that turns socially disaffected young
men into terrorists, and I have myself been tempted to
justify the U.S. government's actions on that basis. But
we must never allow ourselves to be seduced by our fear
into supporting outrageous discrimination and viola-
tions of fundamental American values.

We know that America has signed treaties that prohibit torture and assured the international community
that people we hold for questioning will not endure dehumanizing treatment. Nevertheless, when reports reveal that our government is finding ways to circumvent
these treaties, we simply shrug our shoulders and say,
"They have to do what they have to do to stop these
crazies, who want to kill innocent people." What is
worse is that most of us suspect that there is far more
ugly treatment of prisoners and detainees going on than
we know about.

In reality, we may not want to know what's going on
in places such as Guantánamo Bay. I suspect that the

whole truth, when and if it is revealed, will be too much for any of us to bear. I myself have been tempted to turn away. I can almost hear Jack Nicholson in the movie *A Few Good Men* saying, "You can't handle the truth!" Sometimes I direct that accusation at myself. But I also know that it is only the truth, as Jesus said, that can set me free. I need to know the truth, and I need to respond to the truth as Christ would have me do: I must oppose torture.

In the midst of the ugly attitudes that have arisen since 9/11, you two are going to have to make some decisions about how you will relate to Muslims. I hope you decide to try to be a bridge between the Muslim community and the rest of America. Jesus has called us, according to 2 Corinthians 5:18, to a "ministry of reconciliation." Remember Paul's message to the Athenians on Mars Hill, in which he declared that we are all children of the same God, regardless of our differences (Acts 17:26).

If you're going to accept this challenge, I encourage you to begin by getting to know some Muslim people personally. Consider inviting a Muslim couple to dinner. (Make sure to attend carefully to Islamic dietary laws.) Make the visit an opportunity for them to tell you what they believe and how they practice their religion. You'll be surprised by how much they know about Jesus and all that it says about him in their holy book, the Koran. Just for starters, Muslims believe that Jesus was virgin-born, that he performed miracles (even though there is no claim that Muhammad ever did), and that there will be a Second Coming of Christ. You are likely to learn that only a very small percentage of Muslims are in the Islamic Fundamentalist and threatening movement of which Osama bin Laden is a part. Furthermore, you'll probably be surprised to learn that those practices in sharia law that we find most offensive, such as the stoning to death of homosexuals and adulterous women, are not prescribed in the Koran. Instead, they are practices, as Shi'ite imams like to point out, that are taught in the Old Testament.

Almost every time I have listened carefully to a Muslim explaining Islamic beliefs and practices, he or she has graciously asked me in return to explain what I believe. Such an opportunity to witness for Christ and share my faith has always come when I listened and learned from my Muslim friends first. Too often we speak before we listen, and instead of enjoying a time of mutual sharing, we argue.

In working toward reconciliation with the Islamic world, you must also work to rid yourselves of the kinds of fear I have already described. I know from Scripture that "perfect love casteth out fear" (I John 4:18). Believing this, I also realize that only an unction given by the Holy Spirit can provide me with this special love. This special kind of infilling of the Holy Spirit comes through prayer. As I pointed out in an earlier letter, the praying that infuses me with that love that "casteth out fear" involves more than petitioning God to give me what I need. Instead, as mystical as it might sound, this essential infilling of the Holy Spirit comes to me in what St. Ignatius called "centering prayer." I seek out a quiet place and sit alone, waiting until I am inwardly still. Then I wait patiently for the Spirit to flow into me and saturate me with her presence. This kind of centering prayer, in the words of an old African American spiritual, "makes me love everybody."

Empowered by the Holy Spirit, I am then ready to encounter my Muslim friends. As I listen to them, I can then make a conscious effort to look deeply into their eyes, spiritually and emotionally pouring myself into them. When filled with the Spirit, I am able to connect with people in deeply significant ways and touch them with the love that the Bible calls the "fruit of the Spirit" (Galatians 5:22). This is what Paul was referring to when he tried to explain the difference between knowing someone "in the Spirit" and knowing that person "in the flesh."

I don't mean to minimize the differences between Islam and Christianity. But you must remember that an individual's loving, personal, transforming relationship with a resurrected and ever-present Jesus is more important than his or her membership in a church. Of course, I'm pleased when people join up with us and become members of a church. But many Muslims have come to know and love Jesus in personal and transforming ways while remaining Muslims, just as many Messianic Jews have come to know Jesus while remaining Jewish. This is particularly true of Sufi Muslims. The founder of the Sufi movement so loved Jesus and depended on him for salvation that other Muslims accused him of having become a Christian. They put him to death by crucifixion because they thought that would be a fitting way to be rid of him, given his constant talk of how God's love was revealed in Christ's death on the cross.

It's a strange world out there, and the God that we Red-Letter Christians worship transcends the confines that most Evangelicals theologically prescribe for him. While I am absolutely convinced that "there is no other name under Heaven, whereby we might be saved" (Acts 4:12), I am also convinced that Jesus is alive and touching people who are outside of Christianity and the church. He's really much bigger than we Evangelicals make him out to be.

Lastly, if you wish to truly build a bridge between Christianity and Islam, you must make it a point to stand up for Muslim people whenever they are unjustly described or condemned in private conversations. Martin Luther King Jr. once said, "In the end it will not be the attacks of my enemies that most hurt me, but the silence of my friends." If you are going to be friends with Muslims (and how else can you share Christ's love and salvation with them?), then you cannot remain silent when ugly untruths are spoken in your presence.

Needless to say, it will be hard to follow my suggestions; you will be misunderstood by fellow Christians. But remember these words of Jesus: "Blessed are ye, when men shall revile you, and persecute you, and shall say all manner of evil against you falsely, for my sake" (Matthew 5:11).

Sincerely,
Tony

14

■ Becoming Blessed Peacemakers

Dear Timothy and Junia,

It is important for you to take a stand on war because war seems inescapable in our present age. War has always been and should always be a moral issue for Christians. In America today, it has also become a major *political* issue for Evangelicals.

Evangelicals have been far more supportive of the current war in Iraq than the general U.S. public. Recent polls have shown that the majority of Americans have soured on the war in Iraq and believe that it was a mistake to ever invade that country in the first place. But President Bush knows that he can still depend on Evangelicals to support his war policies.

Because of this, Evangelicals have come under fire for what is perceived as their support of the war. Many critics have pointed out the incompatibility of militarism with our pro-life values. Certainly, observers are right to feel some confusion when an Evangelical organization such as the Southern Baptist Convention takes a strong position against abortion on pro-life grounds but then turns around and gives public approval to the deadly war in Iraq.

Jesus had strong words on the subjects of war and peace, as any honest reader of the Bible—and particularly the Sermon on the Mount (Matthew 5–7)—must acknowledge. In Matthew 5:9, he says, "Blessed are the peacemakers: for they shall be called the children of God." Then, in Matthew 5:38,

> *Ye have heard that it hath been said, An eye for an eye, and a tooth for a tooth: But I say unto you, That ye resist not evil: but whosoever shall smite thee on thy right cheek, turn to him the other also.*

And in Matthew 26:52,

> *Then said Jesus unto him, Put up again thy sword into his place: for all they that take the sword shall perish with the sword.*

The early Christians were pacifists, and most scholars will tell you that the church remained pacifist until the time of Constantine in the early fourth century. Up until then, Christianity had been regarded as little more than an obnoxious Jewish sect whose pacifism ran contrary to the military ideals that served as the foundation of the Roman Empire. But Constantine needed a religion to unite his pluralistic domain. He found that religion in Christianity. In the Jesus of Christianity, he found a God that transcended ethnic and territorial divisions and made humanity one people. Thus, Christianity was made the state religion. In return for this favor, the church provided religious legitimization to Constantine's rule. Along with that legitimization, the church lent support for the army that enabled Constantine to maintain and extend his empire.

Overnight, the armies of Rome were Christianized—at least symbolically. The leader of one Roman legion ordered his soldiers to march into the Mediterranean Sea and stoop under the water for a mass baptism into the church. But, crucially, the general told his troops that as they went under the water, each man should hold up the arm that he used to hold his sword in battle to keep that arm from being baptized. In other words, he wanted his men to be Christians, except when it came to killing the enemies of Rome.

This wedding of Christianity and the Roman Empire was the first of many alliances between our church and the state. Many believe that the church has never fully recovered from the Constantinian compromise. Certainly, the church has struggled with the subject of war ever since, and has come up with all sorts of theologies to justify its militarism.

So far, the theory of "just war" is the best idea to emerge from this struggle. First outlined by St. Augustine in the fourth century and later updated by the Protestant reformer John Calvin, just-war theory has provided a rationale by which even deeply dedicated Christians can march off to war believing that they are doing the will of God. But, importantly, according to just-war theory, they must first consider the nature of the war they are joining because it is only sanctioned if a specific set of criteria applies. The most salient points of just-war theory are:

1. That war is the only means whereby a nation can protect itself.
2. That all alternatives to war have been exhausted.
3. That the good achieved outweighs the evil that is done.
4. That there be an avoidance of civilian casualties.

Personally, I struggle with just-war theory. I'm not convinced that Scripture supports even this limited sanction for military aggression. But these questions are irrelevant in the case of Iraq, because that war certainly doesn't fall within the parameters of just-war theory.

We now know that those weapons of mass destruction that were the pretext for the war were nowhere to be found when our troops got to Iraq. Then, the rhetoric of the government changed and the claim was made that we were removing a dictator and establishing democracy. But when the result has been the creation of a Shi'ite republic wherein the rights of women and the freedom to practice religions other than Islam are limited, that justification no longer flies. Now we are being told that we invaded Iraq to fight terrorists there so that we won't have to fight them here on American soil. This claim is being made in spite of the facts that there were no reported terrorists in Iraq; that Osama bin Laden was in Afghanistan; and that those who flew the planes into the World Trade Center and the Pentagon were from Saudi Arabia and Egypt (our allies!).

Junia and Timothy, most of our Evangelical brothers and sisters go on believing that we entered this war with just cause. They refuse to face the fact that instead of rooting out terrorists, this war has made Iraq into the biggest terrorist training camp in the world—while turning countless previously noncombatant Iraqi civilians into supporters of Al-Qaeda. No wonder many people have become cynical about the official statements justifying this war and are saying that if mushrooms had been Iraq's biggest export instead of oil, we would have never invaded.

It is not clear to me that Iraq posed a direct threat to the safety and well-being of the United States. I am also not convinced that our government had exhausted all of the alternatives to war. Certainly, knowing what we know now, we can see that very little good has come of this war and much evil has been perpetrated. The number of civilian casualties in this war has been enormous, far exceeding the number of combatant casualties. The Brookings Institute estimates that to date as many as *100,000* ordinary Iraqi citizens may have died as a consequence of the American-led invasion of Iraq, and that more than three times that number have been seriously wounded. I cannot understand why all of our Evangelical friends aren't outraged by this.

Life has certainly gotten much worse for Christians in Iraq as a result of the war. Because the coalition forces have been viewed in the Muslim world as being a Christian army, conjuring up despicable images of the medieval Crusades, a wave of anti-Christian feelings has swept over the Muslims in Iraq. Churches are being burned down in Baghdad, and tens of thousands of Christians have been forced to flee the country for fear of persecution. Prior to the invasion, Christians had extensive freedoms in Iraq and were even allowed to evangelize. That is changing now that a Shi'ite government is in place. Under the new regime, women's rights are also becoming increasingly circumscribed.

Beyond the tremendous suffering the war has created for the people of Iraq as well as the families and friends of the thousands of American soldiers who have been killed or maimed by the war, I see another problem that may shape our history for decades to come. I am very concerned about how this war will shape relations between Christians and Muslims in the twenty-first century. I am beginning to take seriously the argument put forward by Harvard scholar Samuel Huntington in his book *The Clash of Civilizations*. Huntington contends that the geopolitics of the future will be marked by wars between the so-called Christian nations of the West and the Islamic world. I hope he's wrong—but there are some frightening signs that he may be right. Already, many Muslim media sources are interpreting the invasion of Iraq as a rebirth of the medieval Crusades. Evangelical missionaries are being pushed out of many Muslim countries, not just Iraq. But our brothers and sisters on the Religious Right do not seem interested in improving our image in the minds of Muslims; instead, a great many of them refer to Islam as an evil religion and call for its destruction.

What this war is costing America is out of sight. Most important is the human cost, as thousands of our finest young men and women have been wounded or killed. Beyond this, the war is costing almost $2 billion a week. Guess who's loaning a good bit of the money to cover this weekly debt? The People's Republic of China! Just think of the implications of that.

In Luke 14:31, Jesus notes that no wise king would go to war unless he was certain that he had the resources to win that war. I wish the decisionmakers in Washington had read and heeded what Jesus said. Those on the Religious Right may be cheering America's militarism.

But like many other socially progressive Evangelicals, I am not.

If you have strong feelings already about the war in Iraq, Timothy and Junia, I think you will find it is essential to have a thoroughly reasoned position on this crucial issue, because your secular friends are very likely to ask you to explain why Evangelicals claim to follow the Prince of Peace and yet rally in support of war.

Given the teachings of Jesus, the pacifism of the early Christians, and the fact that our current war is illegitimate according to the standards of just-war theory, you might be wondering why a large majority of Evangelicals, and almost all Fundamentalists, support George Bush's policy in Iraq. I can't answer this question definitively, but I have some ideas that you might want to consider.

First of all, Evangelicalism has become increasingly patriotic in recent years. Most Evangelicals are convinced that Christianity played a crucial role in creating America and that, consequently, God smiles on America in particular. In the Mayflower Compact, the Pilgrims used a biblical metaphor to describe their enterprise: "a city that is set on a hill cannot be hid" (Matthew 5:14). Many Evangelicals believe that America has lived up to this vow, and that we have been a special people chosen by God to exemplify the values of the kingdom of God here on earth. Defying the facts of history, nationalistic Evangelicals usually make the unabashed claim that our founding fathers intended America to be a Christian nation. Some believe that America is in fact the new Israel, elected by God to bring salvation to the rest of the world.

In this context, you can see how some Evangelicals might believe that America is living out its calling to carry abroad the blessings that God has bestowed on us. War, for many of our people, becomes a holy crusade; in an unguarded moment, our president even called it that. Though we may not actually use the word *crusade*, many Evangelicals do view our wars abroad in those terms, and believe that we engage in war with the idea of ultimately enlightening the peoples we conquer.

Recently, I was driving through southern Georgia when I passed a church that had a large, solid wooden cross on its lawn. Nailed to the top of the cross was a sign that read Support our Troops. Draped over the crossbar was an American flag. I don't think I can come up with a better illustration of how militaristic nationalism has merged with Christianity in the minds of many Evangelicals.

There is another reason, I think, that American Evangelicals have become so vocally pro-war: their strong identification with the Republican Party. As the GOP calls for support for the war in Iraq, Evangelicals too often follow

the party line rather than make their own moral and political judgments. This is not to suggest that the Democratic Party is some kind of peace party. It is not! But the
point must be made that whenever Christianity becomes
identified with *any* political party, it tends to take on the
values of that party, rather than remaining loyal to the
principles of Scripture.

I have spent, and will continue to spend, a great
deal of time thinking about what the Bible tells us
about war. As a result, I believe in nonviolent resistance. I do not call myself a pacifist because I believe
that we ought not to remain passive in the face of evil. I
do believe, however, that we should fight evil in nonviolent ways. That is what Mahatma Gandhi and Martin
Luther King Jr. believed, and I follow their lead. I am
convinced that this is what Jesus meant when he told us
to overcome evil with good. And yet even as I write
this, I remain troubled by my own position. I must acknowledge that my freedom to express these very views
has been paid for with the lives of many heroic American patriots.

You should be aware that those who argue against my position also use Scripture to make their case. They often
point to all the militarism ordained by God in the Hebrew
Bible, and it is certainly true that in those pages we read
about God approving of warfare. However, in the New
Testament, Jesus transcended the old commandment of

"an eye for an eye and a tooth for a tooth." Instead, in Matthew 5:43–44, he said,

> *Ye have heard that it hath been said, Thou shalt love thy neighbour, and hate thine enemy. But I say unto you, Love your enemies, bless them that curse you, do good to them that hate you, and pray for them which despitefully use you, and persecute you.*

Of course, I hope that you will join me in believing that Christianity and militarism don't go together. Gandhi once said, "Everybody understands what Jesus taught—except for Christians." I hope that in the coming months and years, all of our Evangelical brothers and sisters will spend more time thinking about what Jesus taught and less time thinking about what the Republican Party tells us to do.

During my first half hour in Heaven, I will ask whether there is any such thing as a just war. Until then, I will continue to struggle with this question, as I am sure you are doing right now.

Sincerely,
Tony

15

■ Women and the Church

Dear Junia and Timothy,

I want to tell you something vitally important that is too often hidden from Evangelicals: Jesus was a radical feminist! Although it was common in his time to relegate women to a position inferior to men's, Jesus treated them as equals. He invited them to be students of the Torah, which back then was a privilege reserved for men (Matthew 10:35–42). He broke the taboo on touching women when they were menstruating (Mark 5:25–34). He was even willing to transgress ancient Jewish standards of social respectability by establishing relationships with women of questionable ethnic and moral backgrounds (John 4:1–27).

The Scripture tells us that "in Christ there is neither male nor female" and that "all are one in Christ Jesus" (Galatians 3:28). Nevertheless, many feminists get nervous around Evangelical Christians, and for good reason. They never know what to expect when they meet us. Some, like Mary Stewart Van Leeuwen, my colleague at Eastern University, are powerful advocates for women's equality. She and other Evangelical feminists provide convincing biblical support for the claim that Jesus opposed any form of second-class citizenship for women.

But other Evangelicals tend toward a version of Fundamentalism that legitimates the submission of women and leads them to oppose the idea of women's occupying leadership roles within the church. This latter group also relies on Scripture and readily quotes the apostle Paul in Ephesians 5:22–25:

> *Wives, submit yourselves unto your own husbands, as unto the Lord. For the husband is the head of the wife, even as Christ is the head of the church: and he is the savior of the body. Therefore as the church is subject unto Christ, so let the wives be to their own husbands in every thing. Husbands, love your wives, even as Christ also loved the church, and gave himself up for it.*

and 1 Timothy 2:11–12:

> *Let the woman learn in silence with all subjection. But I suffer not a woman to teach, nor to usurp authority over the man, but to be in silence.*

We believe that the Bible is infallible, and some Evangelicals take this to mean that in light of passages such as the ones I've quoted above, there is no wiggle room when it comes to defining the role of women in the home and in the church. But many of us disagree with this logic. The fact that the Bible is infallible does not mean that we have to take every passage of Scripture at face value. That may sound like heresy to most Fundamentalists, but some Evangelicals contend that, in interpreting Scripture, not every verse should be taken literally and certain rules of interpretation should be followed. One primary rule is that we should ask what any given passage meant to the people in the early church who first heard the words.

How, then, do we read these passages? Many Evangelicals cite church historians in explaining that these verses reflect Paul's response to a particular problem that had arisen among first-century Christians. Some Evangelical scholars suggest that some women who became Christians in the early days of the church were quick to abuse the new freedom and equality that they experienced as a product of their spiritual liberation. Some accounts indicate that some women, suddenly allowed to speak out and voice their concerns in religious gatherings, used the opportunity to discuss the ways in which their husbands were failing in their marital responsibilities. Some women, it is conjectured, even lectured their husbands in front of the entire congregation of fellow believers. If that was the case, it is easy to understand why Paul would tell them to remain silent in church and enjoin them to talk to their husbands in the privacy of their homes (I Corinthians 14:34–35).

What about wives submitting to their husbands? There are alternate ways of reading these lines as well. It seems clear to me that *mutual* submission is what is called for in Ephesians 5:22. In fact, many would claim that in the preceding verse, Paul calls upon husbands and wives to submit themselves to *one another* (Ephesians 5:21). Paul goes on to tell husbands to love their wives "even as Christ loved the church and gave himself up for it" (Ephesians 5:25). We know that Christ loved the church by becoming its servant (Philippians 2:7)—in the Greek language, the word is *doulos*, which means "slave." What wife would have any trouble submitting herself to a man who defined himself as her slave? And so, yes, wives are supposed to submit to their husbands, but Scripture also tells us that husbands should submit to their wives.

At this point, you may be asking, "Who, then, is the final authority in the decisionmaking process within the family?" The best answer to that question is *"Christ!"* Within biblical Christianity, husbands and wives are declared to be equals. When faced with difficult decisions, they should join together and prayerfully seek what Christ would have them do. According to Philippians 2:3, each partner should respect the opinions of the other and even give precedence to the other:

> *Let nothing be done through strife or vainglory; but in lowliness of mind let each esteem the other better than themselves.*

I have quoted several passages from Scripture in this letter because those Evangelicals who want to see women subordinated in both home and church constantly quote from Scripture to support their point of view. I want you to be well aware that their biblical case is not as strong as they claim that it is. One can use the very same passages and others to make a strong case for equality and mutuality between the sexes.

Evangelicalism has not always been antifeminist. In fact, Evangelicals provided some of the most significant early support for the women's suffrage movement. As I mentioned in an earlier letter, Charles Finney, the acknowledged "Billy Graham" of the nineteenth century, made feminism a major part of his evangelistic preaching. He proved to be a leading recruiter of workers for the suffrage movement. Some of the earliest meetings of the feminist movement in America were held in Evangelical churches in upstate New York, in part as a result of Finney's preaching. Finney also believed that women should have leadership roles in the church. He played a major role in developing Oberlin Seminary and Oberlin

College, where women were admitted to training courses to prepare them for Christian ministry.

Finney was doing nothing new or unprecedented when he advocated for women in ministry. According to Acts 2:18, God ordained women to prophesy (i.e., preach) from the earliest days of the church, when the Holy Spirit came upon the first-century Christians. We read in Scripture that the apostle Philip had daughters who preached (Acts 21:8–9) and about Euodia and Syntyche, who were leaders in the church at Philippi (Philippians 4:2). Women such as Priscilla played key teaching roles in the spiritual formation of male leaders (Acts 18:26).

Junia and Timothy, if we are going to change the minds of Evangelicals who use the Bible to try to suppress women, then we are going to have to use the Bible to make our case, too.

If you are wondering why I am so strongly committed to supporting women's right to be preachers and leaders, you should know that it is because of my mother. She had all the gifts to be a great preacher. I often watched her at family gatherings holding both young and old in rapt attention with her entertaining stories.

My mother always wanted to be a preacher, but back when she was coming of age, women were kept from taking that role. I am convinced that there is something horribly wrong with preventing someone like my mother from actualizing her God-given gifts and living out her calling from God. Southern Baptists have made a major issue out of taking ordination away from women, and I believe that they are dead wrong. I believe that the Bible clearly teaches the doctrine of the "priesthood of all believers," which means that all Christians, regardless of gender, are ordained by God to all the callings of Christian ministry. I know that you two probably think that this is a no-brainer. It's not! Fundamentalists have made opposition to feminism a prominent part of their present-day agenda. You'll often hear their preachers refer to the feminist movement as being anti-Christian. Defining the family in a hierarchical fashion, with the husband as the head, they condemn any attempt to yield to wives equal authority.

These same Fundamentalists are threatened by anything that even *seems* like it is tending toward feminist thinking, as is evidenced by their upset over the use of inclusive language in church liturgy or in any translation of Scripture. You can count on their outrage in response to any suggestion that God transcends what some of us consider to be culturally prescribed definitions of masculinity. Whenever I preach about the mothering side of God—revealed, for instance, when Jesus talked about wanting to gather people together as a hen gathers her chicks (Matthew 23:37)—I can expect letters of condemnation during the days that follow.

Christian feminists believe that discovering the female side of God has made it easier for them to relate to

God, but more important is the biblical case for affirming God's feminine traits. Consider the fact that when God's spirit is referred to in the Hebrew Bible, a feminine noun is used, and in the original Greek version of the New Testament, the Holy Spirit can be understood as being feminine.

We must zealously affirm women's right to assume leadership roles within the church. These roles were accorded to women in New Testament times, and they should be accorded to them now. We must support women's right to these roles not only because the cause is just, but also because we cannot afford to lose half of the talented people in the church as we embark on the tasks that lie before us in these crucial days. I beg you both to not let up in efforts to ensure women the opportunity to become all that they can be.

Sincerely,
Tony

16

■ Creation Care

Dear Timothy and Junia,

Al Gore, our former vice president, has tried to tell us the truth—that we are destroying our natural habitat in ways that are dangerously threatening to our future. We older folks, however, do not seem especially alarmed as he cites climatologists' warnings about global warming and biologists' predictions of the consequences for all living creatures of our ongoing pollution of land, sea, and air. The good news is that your generation seems more attuned to his message, perhaps because more and more schools are including environmental studies as part of the academic curriculum.

The tragedy of environmental degradation became shockingly clear to me when, more than a decade ago, I stood in the north of Senegal with the chief of a local tribe. We were surveying the impact of an ongoing drought that was then affecting the entire Sahel region of Africa. The chief explained that the drought was killing off the herds of sheep and goats that once had been the primary form of sustenance for his people. He told me about the young men of his tribe who, knowing that there was no future for them as shepherds, were leaving to seek employment in the capital city of Dakar. Then he said, "This is not a drought. The people of my tribe know how to survive droughts. We have done that many times over the years. This is not a drought! The earth is changing!"

Of course he was right. The world is changing, and the changes are the result of human irresponsibility. The rain that usually falls in Senegal comes from clouds that are formed over the jungles of the Amazon in Brazil. Those clouds then move across oceans and deliver rain onto the Sahel region of Africa where that chief and his people lived. But in recent years, the rain forests of Brazil have been destroyed at an incredible rate. Entrepreneurs using chop-and-burn deforestation techniques are turning the Amazon into grazing land for beef cattle. Every hour, an amount of land equivalent to the size of a football field is being deforested. Consequently, the amount of moisture produced in the Amazon decreases each year. That decline is among the factors responsible for what the chief and I observed that hot afternoon as we stood together on the banks of the parched bed of the Senegal River.

One night, on a flight to Argentina, my plane passed over the Amazon. As I looked out of the airplane window, I was awed. As far as I could see, there were fires burning off the jungle to make way for new grazing land. This destruction is the price we are paying to satisfy the world's exponentially growing hunger for beef. As I stared at the fires, I couldn't get my mind off of that African chief and his conviction that the climate of the earth is changing; I realized that this was part of the reason why. Our beef-eating habits are not only leading to clogged arteries, they are also destroying a way of life for a tribe in faraway Africa.

Whenever I bring up my ecological concerns in Evangelical circles, I am fearful of being greeted with suspicion. Right-wing Evangelicals tend to see environmentalists as alarmists who endanger the economic well-being of the country.

Again, I point to the alliance of most Evangelicals with the conservative wing of the Republican Party. I believe that this alliance may be largely responsible for such anti-environmentalist biases. Evangelicals who see President Bush as one of their own born-again brothers support the president's anti-environmentalist policies and his repeated argument that we lack sufficient evidence to prove that global warming is happening.

Political conservatives, for the most part, have some justifiable concerns about the possible economic impact of extensive environmental regulation. They worry that compliance with strict government restrictions on industrial waste and other pollutants will impose a great economic burden on American industry and render it less competitive in the global marketplace.

It was this kind of economic consideration that kept President Bush from signing the Kyoto treaty. This treaty, which was designed to dramatically reduce emissions of carbon dioxide and other atmospheric pollutants, provided certain exemptions to China for several upcoming years. Our president feared that these exemptions would give China an unfair advantage in producing goods for the world market. This, he believed, would not only hurt American business, but also would be to the detriment of all Americans.

Evangelicals are suspicious of environmentalism for other reasons as well. Many Evangelicals believe that environmentalism is part of a New Age movement. But if the New Age movement has been able to make the issue of the environment their own, it is only because the church has put up no resistance and has failed to make environmentalism an important part of its own agenda.

The responsibility to take care of God's creation is prescribed in Scripture. This is clear. In the Hebrew Bible, we read that God requires us to be stewards of creation. We read in the opening chapters of Genesis that God gives to Adam and Eve the responsibility of caring for their natural habitat. Theologians from John Calvin on have made creation care a part of Christian discipleship. In the New Testament, we read such passages as Romans 8:19–22, wherein those who are imbued with the Holy Spirit are expected to reclaim nature from its spoiled condition. It reads,

> For the earnest expectation of the creature waiteth for the manifestation of the sons of God. For the creature was made subject to vanity, not willingly, but by reason of him who hath subjected the same in hope, because the creature itself also shall be delivered from the bondage of corruption into the glorious liberty of the children of God. For we know that the whole creation groaneth and travaileth in pain together until now.

Too many Evangelicals have evaded their responsibility to the environment for far too long. But there are signs that things are changing for the better. Many of us Red-Letter Christians are making the environment one of our primary concerns. For instance, one of the leaders of our movement, Ron Sider, has founded the Evangelical Environmental Network, an organization that is bringing together Evangelicals who share his commitment to environmentalism. Sider is urging us to adopt simpler, less wasteful, and more environmentally responsible lifestyles. This network of

Christians is also lobbying the government to do more to protect our environment against polluters. Evangelicals who take our scriptural mandate seriously should support these initiatives and others like them.

When it comes to caring for creation, we Red-Letter Christians have found special inspiration in the life of St. Francis of Assisi. Francis appreciated the sacredness of nature. His famous *Canticle* captures something of his mystical appreciation of God's creation. It is worth repeating here.

> *O most high, almighty, good Lord God, to thee*
> *   belong praise, glory, honor, and all blessing.*
> *Praised be my Lord God with all creatures and*
> *   especially our brother sun, who brings us the*
> *   day and who brings us the light; fair is he and*
> *   shines with a very great splendor: O Lord, he*
> *   signifies to us Thee.*
> *Praised be my Lord for our sister the moon, and*
> *   for the stars, which he hath set clear and*
> *   lovely in the heavens.*
> *Praised be my Lord for our brother the wind, and*
> *   for the air and cloud, calms and all weather*
> *   by which Thou upholdest life in all creatures.*
> *Praised be my Lord for our sister water, who is*
> *   very serviceable unto us and humble and*
> *   precious and clean.*

Praised be my Lord for our brother fire, through
*   which Thou givest us light in the darkness;*
*   and he is bright and pleasant and very mighty*
*   and strong.*
Praised be my Lord for our mother the earth,
*   which doth sustain us and keep us, and*
*   bringeth forth divers fruits and flowers of*
*   many colors, and grass.*
Praised be my Lord for all those who pardon one
*   another for his love's sake, and who endure*
*   weakness and tribulation; blessed are they who*
*   peaceably shall endure, for Thou, most*
*   Highest, shalt give them a crown.*
Praise ye and bless the Lord and give thanks unto
*   him and serve him with great humility.*

I know that the mysticism implied in this poem will raise some eyebrows among some of our more conservative friends, but we Red-Letter Christians enthusiastically identify with it.

Francis believed that all creatures were created for the explicit purpose of worshipping God. Hence, the annihilation of any species would diminish the adoration that is God's due. He derived such conviction from Psalm 148, which reads,

Praise the Lord from the earth, ye dragons, and all
deeps: fire, and hail; snow, and vapour; stormy wind

fulfilling his word: mountains, and all hills; fruitful
trees, and all cedars: beasts, and all cattle; creeping
things, and flying fowl: kings of the earth, and all
people; princes, and all judges of the earth: both young
men, and maidens; old men, and children: Let them
praise the name of the Lord: for his name alone is
excellent; his glory is above the earth and Heaven.

I, personally, am sensitized to the Franciscan per-
spective on animals each year when my wife and I go
whale watching off the shores of Provincetown, Massachusetts. The naturalist on the boat with us talks
about the decimation of whales and how they are on
the verge of extinction. It is then that I remember that
the psalmist declared that whales were created to sing
hymns of praise to God. Whales sing! At least, hump-
back whales do. What's more, they create new songs
every year. Silencing their voices of worship by anni-
hilating them is sinful. It might even be considered
blasphemous.

I'm encouraged these days, as more and more Evangelicals seem to be recognizing the need to be responsible stewards of God's creation. Recently, the National
Association of Evangelicals, an organization represent-
ing most Evangelical Christians, issued a strong statement calling for members to join together in personal
and political action to protect the environment. Although some of our prominent spokespersons made

noises of opposition, this statement marked a significant shift in a positive direction on this issue.

I must bring up another threat to God's creation, perhaps the gravest threat of all: nuclear proliferation. Right now, in a fearful response to terrorism, we are renewing nuclear-production activities and upgrading nuclear-testing facilities. This only encourages nations such as Iran and North Korea to develop nuclear weapons in response. But the danger posed by those two nations is not as great as the danger posed by terrorists such as Osama bin Laden, who has called it a "religious duty" to secure and use nuclear weapons to destroy Americans. Given that the materials needed to make nuclear weapons exist all over the world, sometimes secured by nothing more than a few guards and a chain-link fence, it is entirely possible that Al-Qaeda terrorists will carry out his wishes.

We Evangelicals, as a people who have been called by Jesus to be peacemakers, should be concerned about the existence of the nuclear threat. The Christian activist William Sloan Coffin Jr. rightly said, "Only God has the authority to end all life on the planet; all we have is the power." I agree with Coffin that it is time for us to give up that power.

In 1968, our nation, along with 42 other nations, signed the Nuclear Non-Proliferation Treaty. As of this writing, 187 nations are parties to the treaty. The signing nations who do not have nuclear weapons have promised to forego developing them provided that the nuclear powers eventually disarm. But instead of honoring our treaty obligations, America and the other nuclear nations have lived by a double standard, assuming the right to deploy nuclear weapons and threatening to do so while forbidding the rest of the world to develop them. It is no wonder that the president of Iran mocks America and tells the rest of the world that, given our failure to live up to the Non-Proliferation Treaty, he has no obligation to stop his country's nuclear-development program.

Most Evangelicals remain indifferent to all of this and support a U.S. military that maintains the nuclear threat. Although Billy Graham has spoken out against nuclear arms, most other prominent Evangelicals support the politics of possessing a nuclear deterrent. I suppose that goes with the recent marriage of Evangelicals and conservative politics.

I hope you two realize the importance of dealing with this matter. It is appalling to me that people who claim to take the Bible seriously fail to act urgently for nuclear disarmament. Those of us who know that Jesus called us to be peacemakers (Matthew 5:9) and warned that those who live by the sword will die by the sword (Matthew 26:52) ought to be at the forefront of the nuclear-disarmament movement. Given what we have learned from Paul—that the weapons of our warfare are not the weapons of this world (2 Corinthians 10:4)—Christians should be setting examples for the rest of the world when it comes to taking the risks that make for peace.

On Armistice Day in 1948, General Omar Nelson Bradley said in a speech,

> *We live in a world of nuclear giants and ethical infants, in a world that has achieved brilliance without wisdom, power without conscience. We have solved the mystery of the atom and forgotten the lessons of the Sermon on the Mount. We know more about war than we know about peace, more about dying than we know about living.*

Sadly, what he said is especially true of those in our Evangelical community. I hope you will work to change that.

Sincerely,
Tony

1 7

▮ Living in Secular America

Dear Timothy and Junia,

When Evangelicals get together, we tend to discuss our shared concerns about the progressive secularization of American society. We've reached a point where any talk about God outside of church is questioned. It is common for people to claim that religion should only be a private thing, but there is no doubt in my mind that our Evangelical faith calls us to bring biblical values into the public sphere. I believe, as I have said in earlier letters, that we are all commissioned as Christians to work toward changing the world into the kind of world God wants it to be.

Stephen Carter, a best-selling author and law scholar at Yale University Law School, makes a convincing argument that the First Amendment to the U.S. Constitution has been wrongly interpreted by many government authorities in ways that drive any semblance of religion, and especially Christianity, out of the public sector. The

First Amendment, which established what is usually referred to as "the separation of church and state," has been used by some overly cautious educational administrators to justify removing anything religious from public schools. U.S. courts have mandated the removal of all religious symbols and displays (e.g., manger scenes) from public property.

Carter points out that the First Amendment was never intended to create a secular society, but only to ensure that no single religion should gain precedence over other religions. He argues that the framers of the Constitution intended to prohibit in America the establishment of a state religion, as has been the case in many European countries as well as certain Muslim countries, such as Arabia and Malaysia. No single religion, according to Carter's understanding of the Constitution, should have favored status or privileges under the laws of the land.

In terms of the removal of all religion from the public sphere, things are not nearly as extreme as many of our Evangelical brothers and sisters would lead you to believe. For instance, many Evangelicals do not realize that President Clinton, early in his first term in office, gave extensive clarification to the Equal Access Act. This act provides several privileges for *all* religious groups that hitherto were deemed questionable. According to this legislation, school authorities must grant the use of school facilities to Christian groups for such gatherings as Bible-club meetings because these groups are guaranteed the same access to school facilities as any other student group. Students even have the legal right to take a course in which they can study the Bible as part of their school curriculum. This special course, which is already designed and operative in several states, reviews the influence of the Bible on Western civilization. These are just two of the existing provisions that allow religion to be brought into public-school life. Simply said, the exclusion of God talk or religious activities from public schools is not as extensive as it is often believed to be.

Many Evangelicals are really bent out of shape because teachers and other paid school officials are not allowed to lead their students in prayer or devotional readings from the Scriptures. This proscription makes perfect sense to me. *All* citizens, regardless of their religious orientations, are paying taxes to pay the salaries of school personnel. It would be unfair to require that people pay the salaries of persons who promote religious beliefs contrary to their own. I'm sure you can see the logic of that argument.

It seems to me that Evangelicals who are concerned about their children not reading the Bible or having prayer time at the start of the school day could easily solve that problem by doing these things at home, before their children leave for school. Most of them don't, and that leaves open the question as to why they are so upset that the school is not doing what they are unwilling to do themselves.

But many Evangelicals remain convinced that schools, not their child-rearing, are the real problem. As a consequence, public-school education has not received much support from Evangelicals. Voices heard on Christian radio and television, resolutions introduced at the annual meetings of our largest Evangelical denomination, and voter guides provided by Evangelical political-action groups regularly express opposition to public education.

There's a lot wrong with the way we educate children these days, but to reduce the problems to the failures of teachers and the removal of prayer and Bible reading at the start of the school day is far too simplistic.

We must all recognize that teachers in public schools have to deal with students whose lives are in upheaval. Many of these students have been traumatized by their parents' divorces. In many inner-city schools, more than half of the children are born into single-parent families. Many children lack the loving support they need to succeed in school.

Teachers face a great many other challenges as well—challenges that Evangelicals often fail to acknowledge. There are numerous forces mitigating against good education, including television. Studies indicate that children in some school districts watch TV for more than six hours a day.

Given all these obstacles, you'd think that Evangelicals would be praising teachers in the public-school system as daring heroes, rather than lambasting them as dangerous secularists.

The most common response of Evangelicals to the problems of our country's broken educational system is to call upon the government to grant vouchers that families can use to pay tuition at Christian schools. I can understand this desire in light of some educators' actions (e.g., unlawfully excluding anything religious from public-school life). But there are serious drawbacks to voucher systems. They take some of the finest students out of public-school classrooms where their influence is greatly needed. Also, the voucher system is likely to lead to further decreases in the money available for public education.

We Christians ought to recognize our obligation to meet the needs of the entire community, not just our own children. We should recognize our responsibility to fund and work for major improvements in public education.

Apart from their effects on the public-education system, I see other real dangers in the voucher system. My concerns have arisen because of what I have observed in Northern Ireland over the past several years. In that part of the United Kingdom, vouchers have led to segregated Protestant and Catholic Schools. That is because Protestant parents send their children to all Protestant schools and the Catholic parents send their children to all Catholic schools. This separation during children's educational years has contributed to the misinformation and prejudices that foster sectarian hostilities.

When I learned about this, I wondered if vouchers here in America would allow various groups that nurture hatred and prejudice to have greater influence on children in our country. Would the members of groups like the Ku Klux Klan and the Aryan Nation be entitled to vouchers that would enable them to set up schools that foster racial hatred? Would the Nation of Islam (the Black Muslims) be allowed to set up schools that would propagate anti-Semitism? I don't know! What I do know is that Horace Mann, who fathered public education in America, saw public schools as a means for furthering what has been called "the great melting pot"—a vision in which the many different peoples of this land come together in harmonious unity. Is that vision dead? Will Evangelicals use the voucher system help to kill it? I just don't know.

The removal of displays of the Ten Commandments from county and state courthouses is also much discussed among Evangelicals concerned about the nation's secularization.

Recently, a judge down in Alabama made himself into a celebrity in many Evangelical circles by insisting that a stone monument bearing the Ten Commandments be placed on the lawn in front of the state courthouse. Groups such as the American Civil Liberties

Union reacted against this, and the case went right up to the federal courts of appeal. Decisions by these higher courts resulted in a removal of the monument. To many Evangelicals, this was evidence of what they believe to be the anti-Christian forces taking over America.

While I, too, am concerned about the secularization of America, I think far too much is being made of the presence or absence of Ten Commandments monuments on public property. My problem with the big hullabaloo over displaying the Ten Commandments in or around our court buildings is that I don't think they are a good expression of what we as Americans, or even as Christians, really believe. Consider the commandment to "remember the Sabbath Day, to keep it holy" (Exodus 20:8). Unless you are a conservative or Orthodox Jew or a Seventh-day Adventist, you probably don't do that. The biblical Sabbath is Saturday, and the overwhelming majority of Evangelicals who are hot and bothered about the removal of the Ten Commandments from courthouses do not observe it.

The tenth commandment is another one that would have to be recast to gain the acceptance of most modern Evangelicals. You probably remember that the tenth commandment prohibits coveting your neighbor's property—including his house, his ox, his ass, his manservant, his maidservant, and his wife (Exodus 20:17). This commandment designates a wife as the property of her husband—there she is, right along with her husband's ox and ass. That's not the way enlightened Christians think about women.

Then there's the commandment that forbids any "graven images" of God (Exodus 20:4). The early Puritans, in obedience to this commandment, would not allow pictures of Jesus to be displayed in their churches or meeting houses. That's not the rule in our present-day Evangelical churches, where pictures of Jesus are exceedingly common. We have no problem with the graven images of God on the ceiling of the Sistine Chapel or in our own stained-glass windows. Furthermore, we flocked to see Mel Gibson's *The Passion of the Christ* in spite of the fact that the graven image of Jesus on the silver screen could easily be interpreted as a violation of this commandment.

We cannot leave this subject of the Ten Commandments without giving some consideration to the first of them, which demands that we have no other god before our God. There is no doubt that this commandment refers to the God who led the children of Israel out of Egypt and into the Promised Land. This is the God that we Christians believe was incarnated 2,000 years ago in Jesus of Nazareth.

In a pluralistic society that supposedly gives no preference to any one religion, what right do we have to tell non-Christians in America's courtrooms that they ought to give our God preeminence over their gods? Why should Hindu believers, Sikhs, and others have to put up with that? I agree that religion has a place in the public square, but, in accord with the Constitution, I am convinced that no particular faith is entitled to superior or exclusive standing in those places that belong to all Americans.

The controversy over the Ten Commandments in the courtroom touches on a much broader problem within the Evangelical community. Far too many Evangelicals are convinced that America was founded as a Christian nation. Likewise, many of our brothers and sisters in the community of faith declare that our founding fathers were deeply spiritual Christians.

Both of these claims are false. While it is certainly true that the culture of America was highly influenced by Christianity during the Revolutionary and early national periods, the founders of our nation made it a basic principle that neither Christianity nor any other religion would ever be designated as the official religion of our country. Christian values provided a basis for the high humanistic values that are inherent in our national character, but it is wrong to call America a Christian nation. It can easily be argued that our concept of democracy was derived as much from the philosophies of the Enlightenment as from the Bible. In fact, historians tell us that less than 15 percent of those living here in 1776 were members of any church.

Any study of the key framers of the Declaration of Independence and the Constitution will reveal that deists and ethical humanists were among the most prominent signers. Benjamin Franklin can hardly be called a Christian in any traditional sense. Certainly his lifestyle, which included common-law wives and children born out of wedlock, fails to measure up to what most Evangelicals believe is Christian. Thomas Jefferson proves to be no better. His own published version of the Bible cuts out all references to the miraculous (including Christ's resurrection), revealing a religiosity that is beyond the pale of traditional Christian faith. Jefferson's lifestyle, which included the oppressive use of an African American slave as his mistress, contradicts any conventional standard of Christian morality.

I don't want to disrespect these important figures in American history. But I do want to demythologize them and remove them from that realm of sainthood where many Evangelicals place them. To parade them as committed Christians whose lives we should imitate entails some imaginative stretching of the truth, to say the least.

Of course, committed Christians *did* play an important role in the founding of our nation. The Presbyterian minister John Witherspoon signed the Declaration of Independence. The first Speaker of the House of Representatives was another clergyman, Frederick Augustus Conrad Muhlenberg. The reality is that the founders of our country were a mixed bag of Christians, agnostics, deists, and others. It was a pluralistic group—as the American population is today.

Whenever I hear my Evangelical friends say they want to create an America that lives by the values of our founding fathers, I shudder a bit. Many of those founding fathers believed in slavery and denied women equal social and legal status with men. We've come a long way in our understanding of human rights since then. While it is obvious that our country has need for a moral revival, it is simply bad history to paint in glowing colors a flawless version of our past.

When considering secularization, you really must go deeper than the removal of religious symbols and practices from the public domain. Secularization really involves the loss of an awareness of the sacred in everyday life. For most people, religious experiences (if they exist at all) are limited to what happens in church or in rare moments of spiritual consciousness and nurtured in times of crisis or in moments of unusual inspiration.

Few of us regularly think about God as we go about our everyday activities. By contrast, people in preliterate societies often sensed some kind of spiritual presence in everything. The changing of the seasons, the lightning in thunderstorms, the growing of crops, the blowing of the winds . . . all were thought to be the works of spiritual forces.

Over the years, we who have been secularized have come to view things scientifically and rationally, leaving little room for the miraculous. Friedrich Nietzsche, the famed atheistic existentialist, once said, "[God] is dead!

And we have killed him!" By which he meant that our rationalistic approach to the world had demystified it, leaving little room for anything that required belief in the supernatural. Modernity has made us spiritually homeless. We have become a people who have no sense of being situated in a divine scheme. Increasingly, we are a people who suffer from a deadness of the soul; a part of us has starved to death from lack of spiritual nourishment.

We have become skeptical about the possibility of miracles, even when we desperately need them. Around us there appear hollow, empty faces devoid of the ecstasy that only can come from a divine inspiration that transcends our modern worldview.

I am convinced that the reason there is upset over such things as an end to prayer in the public schools and the removal of the Ten Commandments from courtrooms is that they are reminders of the disappearance of the sacred from our everyday lives.

Yet we retain an inkling of realities that cannot be reduced to what we can perceive with our five senses. We have had to pay a high price for living in a secularized world, perhaps too high. Those of your friends who have not wrestled with God in the wee hours of the morning nor encountered the Spirit who can invade us from beyond our three-dimensional universe may dismiss encounters with sacredness as illusionary. But, nevertheless, they are likely to have an unarticulated hunger for something they cannot name that could enliven their souls.

When Evangelical preachers decry secularization, they seldom address these more profound effects of living in a positivist world. It is no wonder that secularists mock those preachers as being superficial and turn away from their sermons. Hungry souls look for bread from Heaven, but often all they receive are stones from pulpits. People long to learn how to avail themselves of that spiritual infilling that can come through prayerful surrender to the ever-present, living Christ. Preachers need to tell them that they should go to a still place and "center down" within themselves, concentrating on the presence of Christ while waiting with pleading hearts and minds for his spirit to invade and saturate their souls. Timothy and Junia, you are called to model this for them. It is the only cure for the spiritual malady brought on by secularization.

Sincerely,
Tony

18

■ Escaping the American Babylon

Dear Timothy and Junia,

I know you share my commitment to communicating the Gospel to those who live secular lives. To do that, you're going to need to adapt your words and style of communication to make them understandable and attractive to those who live outside the church. In short, you are going to have to package the Gospel story in ways that fit in with the social and psychological needs and interests of secularists. I wonder, however, whether in the process of making our message relevant to American secularists, we Evangelicals may have lost some of the essence of biblical Christianity. I worry about this because, in trying to adapt to secularists' ways, we can easily be seduced into their lifestyles and values rather than converting them to ours. Secular society has an array of pseudoreligions that look like Christianity but can lead us away from Jesus.

My first concern is one I alluded to before. It is Evangelicals' tendency to be overly patriotic. We have to ask, is hyper-nationalism so prevalent among our people that it has become a religion of its own, subtly pushing Christianity aside? I love America. It is the best Babylon on the face of the earth. But it is still Babylon! I suppose I should explain what I mean by that statement.

In the book of Revelation, chapters 17 through 21, there is an extensive discourse on the struggles between two cities: Babylon and Jerusalem. Most biblical scholars agree that "Babylon," as it is used in the book of Revelation, was a code name for the Roman Empire. It referred to the dominant socioeconomic system and culture in which early Christians lived out their faith. Because the empire treated criticism as subversive and punished those responsible for such subversion by death, it became common among first-century Christians to use a code name when referring to it.

Over and against the dominant culture called Babylon stood the people of God and the new social order that they were creating in the midst of the old order. This alternative society was nicknamed "the New Jerusalem" (Revelation 21:2). You can glimpse the lifestyle of the Christians who viewed themselves as citizens of this new society in Acts 2. We know from this passage of Scripture that early Christians shared their material resources so that no one was left in need, and that they lived by a radical commitment to the Sermon on the Mount (Matthew 5–7). And while they lived as peaceful and law-abiding citizens, they refused to follow the prevailing nationalistic idolatry of Caesar because their ultimate allegiance belonged to their Lord, Jesus Christ.

"Babylon" can represent *any* socioeconomic or cultural system in which Christians find themselves living out their faith. For instance, Christians in Germany should think of the German societal system as Babylon. Christians in Korea should think the same about their particular socioeconomic system. And, needless to say, Christians in the United States ought to recognize that the American social order, with all of its values, is our Babylon. In this light, interpreting the biblical text is easy.

The first thing to note about Babylon, as defined by John, the writer of Revelation, is that it is a whore (Revelation 17:5). That ugly term is employed to refer to Babylon's destructively seductive power. Certainly, when you take a good look at our consumerist culture, you can see how easily we in America are seduced into its prescribed lifestyle. We exhaust ourselves and all of our resources in buying what the system is ceaselessly trying to sell us, most of which we do not need. Advertising, with its pervasive use of sex as a marketing tool, lures us into believing that our ultimate desires will be gratified by the purchase of goods available in our shopping malls. So effective are the seductive allurements of "the whore" that we, along with the people all around us, have allowed materialism to become our raison d'être. We fail to hear the voice of the Old Testament prophet who asked, "Wherefore do ye spend money for that which is not bread? And your labor for that which satisfieth not?" (Isaiah 55:2).

The second characteristic of Babylon is that she demands that her people worship her (Revelation 13:4). Such idolatry was obvious in the first century, when citizens of the Roman Empire were required to give religious homage to statues of Caesar. But it is less obvious in twenty-first-century America, where idolatry can be disguised as superpatriotism, which many Evangelicals view as a virtue.

When our young people march off to war simply because they are told it is their patriotic duty, without weighing the justice of our nation's cause, have they not given their ultimate allegiance to the state rather than to Christ? Whenever anyone says, "My country, may she always be right; but right or wrong, my country!" is that not an idolatrous statement? When Evangelicals see little difference between the American way of life and the way of life prescribed by the New Testament, have we not crossed the border into the idolatrous city of Babylon?

The Jesus described on all too many Evangelical television shows and pulpits is a white, Anglo-Saxon, Protestant American. Instead of seeing all people on earth as being created in God's image, we Americans seem to have recreated God in our own image. Too many of us make God into a deity who looks just like us and incarnates our values. And because the God we've created is exactly like us and affirms how we live, we seem comfortable with the wasteful affluence of our society. What's worse is that we denounce as heretics any who question the ways and values prescribed by our Babylon.

Thirdly, many Christians will not face the reality that our Babylon, like every Babylon since the one described in the book of Revelation, is doomed to collapse. We will be doomed by our relentless consumerism. Like the biblical Babylon, America will be destroyed as we continue to exhaust the natural resources essential to our survival. In Revelation 18:12–13, John lists all that the people of Babylon consume. In verses 18 and 19, he goes on to say,

> *And they cried when they saw the smoke of her burning, saying,*
> *"What city is like unto this great city!" And they cast dust on their heads, and cried, weeping and wailing, saying, "Alas, that great city, wherein were made rich all that had ships in the sea by reason of her costliness! For in one hour is she made desolate."*

Environmentalists and economists have been trying to convince us that we cannot go on using up nonrenewable natural resources; polluting the earth, the oceans, and the air; and spending money we do not have to buy what we do not need without reaching a point where our whole socioeconomic system collapses. So many of us Evangelicals ignore such problems and blithely go on declaring that global warming is a myth; that America will always come up with the technology necessary not only to maintain, but also to improve, our affluent lifestyles; and that our empire will last for at least a thousand years.

Recently, a friend of mine attended an evening program of entertainment at the Christian school his children attend. In one part of the program, children recited parts of historic American documents and speeches. After each recitation, the students shouted out in unison, "America will live forever!" That litany had the ring of idolatry to it, and it frightened my friend. It sounded far too similar to repetitious nationalistic declarations he had heard in other places and times. He thought of the chanting at the Nuremberg rallies some seventy years ago.

Our drift toward idolatrous nationalism is not my only concern about the future of Evangelicalism in America. I also worry that we Evangelicals could become spoiled by our own fame and success. When Miss America tells television audiences that she is a born-again Christian and that Jesus is the one who made her successful; when NFL players point to Heaven after scoring touchdowns and gather in the middle of the playing field at the end of games to testify to their faith by kneeling in prayer; and when millionaires give testimonies and write books explaining how trust in Jesus enabled them to get rich; I get very nervous. I'm not quite sure how famous Evangelicals' expressions of triumph jive with 1 Corinthians 1:27–28:

> *But God hath chosen the foolish things of the world to*
> *confound the wise; and God hath chosen the weak*
> *things of the world to confound the things which are*
> *mighty; and base things of the world, and things*
> *which are despised, hath God chosen, yea, and things*
> *which are not, to bring to nought things that are.*

I wonder how all of the religious posturing of professional football players harmonizes with the Jesus who said in Matthew 6:5–6 that we should not be like those hypocrites who make a show of their praying, but instead go into a closet, shut the door, and pray in secret. It all makes me wonder whether we no longer think that being a Christian is about taking up the cross and following Jesus in humble servitude. Instead, we've made following Jesus into a "cool thing" that gives the rest of the world the impression that we Evangelicals are quite pleased with how wonderfully superior we are.

That we are growing in number, expanding our power in the halls of government, and enjoying unprecedented wealth and prestige may not prove to be such great blessings. In Revelation 3:16–17, the Lord of History says to a church that has all of these so-called blessings,

> *So then because thou art lukewarm, and neither cold nor hot, I will spue thee out of my mouth. Because thou sayest, I am rich, and increased with goods, and have need of nothing; and knowest not that thou art wretched, and miserable, and poor, and blind, and naked . . .*

Jesus warned, "Woe unto you, when all men speak well of you!" (Luke 6:26). Do the successes we enjoy, the accolades given to us on Fox News, and the honoring of our leaders by various chambers of commerce indicate that we have compromised too much with the dominant culture? Have we baptized the values of our dominant culture and then had the audacity to call these values Christian?

In successfully adopting the communication techniques of the world—for example, putting the Gospel message to the best rock music, discussing Christian life on congenial TV chat shows that imitate *The Tonight Show*, and recasting Christian love into best-selling romance novels—are we losing something unique and preciously radical about Christianity? What if Marshall McLuhan was right, and the media is the message? What if the media we employ to tell the world about Jesus has itself *become* our message? Have we made the message of the cross into something entertaining, its propagators rock stars and TV personalities rather than followers of the One who was forsaken, rejected, and without any comeliness that we should desire him (Isaiah 53:2–3)? In order to increase church membership, have we watered down the hard things Jesus required of his disciples?

When Jesus spelled out what was required of those who follow him, he alienated people. He drove them away by the thousands. And when he asked the twelve whom we've called apostles why they had not also left him, Peter answered that they would have left, except that they had nowhere else to go to find eternal life (John 6:68).

What would happen to the attendance figures at our churches if Evangelical preachers followed in the footsteps of Jesus by calling their members to deny themselves (Luke 9:23), to sell all they have and give to the poor (Mark 10:21)?

What if we took seriously Jesus's warning to his disciples that it is harder for a rich man to enter the kingdom of Heaven than for a camel to go through the eye of a needle (Matthew 19:24)?

How would Evangelicals respond if their churches taught people to take literally the tactics of nonviolence taught by Jesus, including turning the other cheek and overcoming evil with good?

In cities where muggings are common, do our people really want to hear that if someone wants to rip off your coat, you should "let him have your cloak also" (Matthew 5:40)?

How would our fellow Evangelicals respond in times of war to sermons that forcefully declared that those who take up the sword will die by the sword (Matthew 26:52)?

If we Evangelical preachers really preached the cross that followers of Jesus are called to carry, would our churches continue to grow? We tell our people that Jesus will enable them to have successful marriages, to raise happy children, and to be psychologically healthy and socially adjusted in the workplace. But do we tell them what discipleship, as spelled out by Jesus, will cost?

Albert Einstein once said, "What really counts cannot be counted!" We need to pay attention to that statement. We usually mark our success by counting the growing number of people who call themselves Evangelicals. But it may be that, while we are racking up numerical gains, we are losing our souls. In attracting crowds, are we transforming the hard requirements of Jesus into something more palatable?

One of my students at Eastern University became convinced that the radical requisites laid down by Jesus were something he should live out in the here and now. Upon leaving school, he and some like-minded friends went to live in one of the poorest and most derelict neighborhoods of Philadelphia. They wanted to be where they could reach out to some of the neediest people in America. Living in extreme simplicity, he and his friends made food available to people who were hungry, became friends with drug addicts and prostitutes, and mentored children whose lives were so difficult that their hopes and dreams should have long ago been crushed. He and his friends told me that they were simply doing what Jesus asks all of us to do. I'm still troubled by that statement, and by the challenge that it posed—as well I should be.

Another friend of mine who took Jesus's words seriously gave up a lucrative law practice to spend his life helping poor people obtain decent housing. One day, his wealthy brother confronted him by saying, "Look at what you're doing with your life." The brother went on to say, "Don't get me wrong. I believe in being a Christian, up to a point." Before he could say anything else, my friend responded by asking, "Could that point be the cross?"

My final fear for our future is the tendency for Evangelicalism to revert to legalistic Fundamentalism. I see this tendency in many quarters, but especially among those church traditions closest to me. I'm a Baptist, and in both the Southern Baptist Convention and my own branch of the Baptist movement, the American Baptist Churches, USA, I see dramatic evidence of Fundamentalist takeovers.

Among Southern Baptists, the takeover is almost complete. Through brilliant political maneuvering within their denomination, Southern Baptist Fundamentalists have gained control of all of the major state and national offices. Many of the denomination's colleges, universities, and seminaries have lost or are close to losing academic freedom, as Fundamentalists, who now have the majorities on their boards of trustees, are requiring faculty members to adhere to rigid doctrines and practices. The inerrancy of Scripture is the prime concern of these Fundamentalists, and those who are not inerrantists, even if they believe the Bible to be an infallible guide for faith and practice, are forced out of Southern Baptist institutions.

One of the historic principles of the Baptist faith is something known as "soul freedom," which refers to the freedom of individuals to determine what they believe God is revealing to them through Scripture. However, in the wake of the Fundamentalist takeover of the Southern Baptist Convention, this principle has been set aside. Those who teach, preach, or administer in Southern Baptist institutions must now sign doctrinal statements with a strong emphasis on inerrancy if they want to hold on to their positions. Longstanding faculty members at Southern Baptist colleges have been dismissed. Missionaries have had to resign. Denominational leaders have been forced out of office. The narrowness of this Fundamentalism was made evident when one high-ranking denominational officer in the Southern Baptist Convention who admitted to "praying in tongues" in private prayer was asked to either give up the practice or leave his leadership role. The most prestigious Southern Baptist seminary in Louisville, Kentucky, has gone so far as to require strict adherence to the basic teachings of John Calvin as the standard for theological orthodoxy. Those who cannot toe the line are asked to resign. Needless to say, there has been a lot of hurt and meanness as the Fundamentalists have taken over this denomination.

My own denomination, the American Baptist Churches, USA, has not escaped the painful struggles that go with Fundamentalists' flexing their political muscles in efforts to enforce conformity on member churches. Here, the core issue is whether "welcoming and affirming churches" should be allowed to remain a part of our denomination. Welcoming and affirming churches are congregations that have gone on record as being willing to accept as members all persons without regard to their sexual orientation. Because many of these churches accept homosexual marriages and are ready to accept gays and lesbians into the ordained ministry, most in the denomination argue that these congregations have departed from the biblical basis that should guide all Baptist churches.

It is not surprising that most Baptists disagree with the position of welcoming and affirming churches with regard to homosexuality. But another historic principle, one just as basic to being Baptist as soul freedom, may be violated if these welcoming and affirming churches are forced out of the denomination. That principle is the autonomy of the local church. In simple language, that means that no decisionmaking body that transcends the local congregation has the right to determine what the faith and practices of a local church should be. According to this principle, once it has affirmed that Jesus Christ is Lord, Savior, and God, each local church has the right to follow the Spirit's leading and make its own rules. As I mentioned earlier, my wife, who believes that homosexual marriages are permissible, belongs to a Baptist congregation that is welcoming and affirming. Because I do not believe that gay marriages fit in with biblical teachings, I belong to another church. In spite of their differences, both of our churches belong to the same local and national Baptist organizations, and our respective pastors are friends.

Obviously, such church polity allows for diversity among the churches within our denomination, but that diversity is now being challenged. Because our national leaders have been unwilling to yield to the Fundamentalists' demands that all welcoming and affirming churches be put out of the denomination, hundreds of their churches are withdrawing from the American Baptist Churches and forming new denominations.

While it was the question of homosexuality that initiated the struggle, the Fundamentalists are also concerned with what they see as a loss of evangelistic zeal within the denomination. There is some evidence to support the validity of this last accusation, but pulling out of the denomination is not the solution to the problem.

What is happening among Baptists is happening in just about every other mainline denomination, as Evangelicals are slowly but surely moving into alliances with a narrow Fundamentalism that demands conformity in faith and practice. Churches that are independent of denominational affiliations are caught up in the same struggles. Radio and television preachers are constantly rallying their listeners to put pressure on preachers and congregations to adhere to Fundamentalist principles or else be labeled as "liberal"— which is now a term of abuse.

Martin Marty, a church historian at the University of Chicago Divinity School, has made an exhaustive study of Fundamentalism, which he sees emerging in all religions around the world. Indeed, most of us have witnessed the growth of Fundamentalism and have been horrified at the extremism of Jewish and Muslim Fundamentalists in the Middle East; Hindu and Muslim Fundamentalists in India and Pakistan; and Buddhist Fundamentalists in Myanmar. According to Marty, Fundamentalism is an expected reaction to the anomie that comes with social disorganization. When social institutions become shaky, and uncertainty about the future becomes widespread, people look to religion to provide absolutes and a sense of security in the midst of their changing world. There is something to that old gospel hymn that goes, "When rust and decay, all around I see, oh thou who changest not, abide with me." When society seems to be changing too quickly for people to handle, a religion filled with unshakable absolutes becomes very attractive.

It is no surprise to Marty, therefore, that Fundamentalism is experiencing a renaissance here in the United States. It is clear that America's social institutions are in bad shape. Almost half of the marriages that take place in a given year are doomed to divorce. Huge scandals such as those at Enron and WorldCom have left us more suspicious than ever of our commercial institutions. The educational system seems to be broken, and the scandals fermented by religious leaders have caused us to doubt the efficacy of the church. The assault on our moral values by the popular media has left us more than nervous.

In the midst of such social disintegration, people are drawn to Fundamentalism, with its simple but authoritarian answers to the confusing problems that seem to be popping up everywhere. Fundamentalists possess a certainty that perplexed people find powerfully attractive. Evangelicals, who emerged from Fundamentalism to be more free-thinking and less bound by religious legalism, are now struggling to maintain their identity. Increasingly, Evangelicalism shows signs of falling back into a narrow Fundamentalism—so much so that many people see little difference between Evangelicals and Fundamentalists.

Timothy and Junia, hear me on this! If Evangelicalism re-converges with Fundamentalism, our congregations may continue to grow, but we will have lost our heart and soul. And what does organizational success matter if the Spirit of Christ, which is marked by freedom and creative thinking, dies within us? The future of Evangelicalism is in your hands. Don't blow it by yielding to the lure of Fundamentalism.

Sincerely,
Tony

19

■ A Work Ethic for Evangelical Radicals

Dear Junia and Timothy,

I hope this letter finds you healthy in mind, soul, and strength and ready to be challenged—because challenging you is what I hope to do in this letter. I am going to do my best to convince you that being an Evangelical Christian is a full-time calling that requires a sacrificial lifestyle. It is not just something to do in your spare time or when you're not into your "real," workaday job.

One reason we Evangelicals do not have monasteries is that we seek to make the whole world into our monastery. The sacred life, for us, is not a life that involves leaving the secular world and living separately unto God, as Catholic monks usually do. Evangelicals see no division between the sacred and secular spheres of life. We believe that there is one world into which we are called by God to live out sacred vocations.

Work plays an essential role in the life of every Evangelical. You should view your job as a vocation through which your talents can be maximized to meet the needs of others and help change the world into the kind of world God wants it to be. To illustrate this point, let me share a story told to me by a friend of mine who serves as a pastor of a church in Bel-Air, California. It's a wonderful example of how a person in a seemingly mundane vocation interpreted her life as an opportunity for full-time ministry.

My friend told me that she pretends to go shopping each Christmas season in the Nordstrom department store located in her wealthy Los Angeles suburb. I say that she "pretends to go shopping" at Nordstrom because the store is so upscale that she rarely purchases anything there. But she goes there during the Christmas-shopping days because the ambience is spectacular. My friend gets herself a Nordstrom shopping bag, fills it with tissue paper, and meanders around the store, enjoying the decorations and listening to the live music playing in each department.

On one of these Christmas visits to Nordstrom, she was on the top floor, where the most expensive dresses were for sale, when the doors of the elevator opened and a bag lady from off the streets stepped out. When my friend saw this woman, she fully expected that a couple of security guards would show up momentarily to usher the woman out of the store. After all, this woman, whose raggedy clothes were covered with dirt from the streets, was not the kind of person who could afford to buy much of anything at Nordstrom, let alone one of the expensive dresses for sale on the top floor. But instead of security guards, a tall, stately saleswoman appeared and went up the homeless woman. She asked, "Can I help you, Madam?"

"Yeah!" said the homeless woman in a gruff voice. "I want a dress!"

"What kind of dress?" inquired the saleswoman.

"A party dress," was the answer.

"You've come to the right place," the saleswoman replied. "We have the finest dresses in the world."

Indeed they did! The least expensive dress on the rack of evening gowns cost just under a thousand dollars.

The two women looked over the dresses as they talked about which color would be best, given the homeless woman's coloring. After a discussion that went on for more than ten minutes, they picked two dresses off the rack. Then the saleswoman said, "Follow me, Madam. I want you to try on these dresses to see how you look in each of them."

My friend was flabbergasted. She knew the saleswoman must have realized that this homeless woman didn't have the means to buy any of the dresses for sale in the store.

When the two women went into the dressing room to try on the dresses, my friend went into the dressing booth next to theirs and put her ear against the wall so she could listen to what they said. After a while, she heard the homeless woman say, "I've changed my mind. I'm not going to buy a dress today."

The saleswoman answered, "That's quite all right, Madam, but I'd like you to take my card. Should you come back to Nordstrom, I would consider it both a privilege and a pleasure to wait on you again."

My friend was more than surprised by the kind and respectful way in which this saleswoman treated a woman who obviously had not the means to buy anything in that upscale store. This saleswoman did what a Christian should do. In all probability, she treated everyone she met in her everyday encounters in the work place as Jesus would treat them. In what she said and did, we have an example of how a job can become more than a job. We see here that what might be deemed an ordinary vocation can become an extraordinary way in which to live out a calling from God.

Most Christians believe that only pastors and missionaries have received a special calling from God. Ordination for the ministry or the priesthood supposedly sets a person apart from other Christians and gives that person some kind of superspiritual status.

We Evangelicals, on the other hand, question the idea that ordination provides any kind of superior designation of Christian service. Our theology declares that we are a "priesthood of all believers" (Peter 2:9). We believe that each and every one of us is ordained for ministry. That is how we interpret what Paul wrote in Ephesians 2:10: "For we are his workmanship, created in Christ Jesus unto good works, which God hath before ordained that we should walk in them."

You should give as much prayerful consideration to choosing what others may call a secular vocation as missionaries or ministers give to choosing their callings to Christian service. As you consider your decision about a vocation, ask others in your church or support group to prayerfully join you in the process. Seek confirmation from these fellow Christians about whether you are choosing the right path. Too many of us make these decisions on our own, without consulting those who know and love us. If they are honest with us, they can help us see whether we have the gifts and temperament for the vocation being considered.

I cannot stress enough how important it is for you to seek out a vocation that is right for you. Every part of your life will be conditioned by what happens to you in the workplace and the extent to which you find meaningful service to God in your work. In his book *The Art of Loving*, the psychologist and philosopher Erich Fromm contends that a person's everyday life can help energize him or her for humanizing relationships with others. Creative work that allows you to utilize your God-given gifts can give you a sense of fulfillment. The emotional gratification that can come from meaningful work in which you actualize your potential and utilize your talents will generate within you the spiritual and psychic energy to lovingly connect with others.

To love requires spiritual energy, and creativity in our everyday labors plays a significant role in providing that energy. You won't have to look far and wide to find people whose jobs dehumanize them and render them incapable of loving. People's souls are debilitated when they are treated poorly in the workplace, see what they do as meaninglessness, and are unable to exercise their God-given gifts. So many people die before they're dead because their work leaves them hollow. To the extent possible, make sure that your vocation so turns you on spiritually that at the end of the workday you will be fully alive and driven to give yourself away in love. I can't emphasize this strongly enough.

When I explain that each Christian should choose his or her vocation prayerfully, I am often asked, "But what about those who aren't given the privilege of choice? What do you say to those who have to stay in jobs that frustrate them because these jobs are the only way they can support their families? Don't many Christians find themselves trapped in jobs that can diminish their humanity and seem to be meaningless?"

It's certainly true that many Christians find themselves in jobs that they wouldn't have chosen and that are difficult to interpret as divinely appointed vocations. There are some things a Christian should do to make the best of such situations.

First of all, if you find yourself trapped in a job that is hard on your soul, you should nevertheless make a commitment to doing the job well. We learn in Scripture that others will think more or less of the Christ we serve because of the ways we conduct ourselves in the workplace. We should do what we have to do in such a way that, in biblical language, "They will see our good works and glorify the Father who is in heaven" (Matthew 5:16). We are further instructed to work diligently—and not just when the boss is looking on (Ephesians 6:5–6). Diligence at work is a good testimony to the faith that is within us. St. Francis would say, "We should witness for Christ all day long, and sometimes we should use words."

Secondly, you ought to work hard to create a working atmosphere that lifts the spirits of your fellow workers. Whenever possible, your presence in the workplace should be a source of joy for others. Others should be able to look forward to being with you. One of my colleagues tells a story that illustrates this point better than I can.

One night, my colleague preached at a city mission that provides meals and beds for the homeless. At the end of his sermon, he had an altar call, and several men came forward and knelt in prayer. One of the men who knelt at the altar started to cry out to heaven, "Oh, God! Make me like Joe! Oh, God! Make me like Joe!"

Joe was the janitor at the mission and was deeply loved by everyone. There was no task that he considered beneath him. Joe was the one who could be counted on to clean up the vomit or scrub the toilets. And he always did what had to be done with a song. The moment Joe walked into a room, he lit up the place with his contagious smile. He treated homeless derelicts like hotel guests at the Ritz and always went out of his way to provide an encouraging word to the depressed men who came through the doors of that little gospel mission. So it was no surprise that this man at the altar should cry out to God to make him like Joe. My colleague, hearing this, leaned over and whispered in the man's ear, "It really would be better if you prayed, 'Make me like Jesus!'"

With that, the man looked up at my friend and slowly asked, "Is he like Joe?"

That man didn't know much about Jesus, but he did know a great deal about Joe. Joe had given the man an inkling of what Jesus was all about.

Joe took a menial job in a difficult place and made that place into an outpost of the kingdom of God, where God's will was done on earth as it is in Heaven. Every Christian worker should try to do this in his or her own workplace. Joe humanized a Bowery mission that otherwise might have been humiliating and psychologically debilitating. He turned the mundane into something sublime.

My final bit of advice to Christians who find themselves stuck in menial or unsatisfying jobs is that you should try to see the broader significance of what you're doing. Recognizing that one's job contributes to something of great importance to God can do much to make that job meaningful.

Christopher Wren, the British architect who designed London's St. Paul's Cathedral, once toured the cathedral site during construction to talk to the various artisans working there about how things were progressing. He talked to masons, carpenters, sculptors, and stained-glass artists. As he was finishing his tour, Wren came upon an old man whose job was to stir cement with his shovel to keep the cement from hardening. When the great architect asked the man what he was doing, the man, not knowing it was Christopher Wren who was asking, answered, "Why, sir, I'm building a great cathedral to the glory of God."

This man had found meaning in his job by understanding it as a part of something much bigger. He had discovered a way to make what could have been a humdrum task into meaningful work.

Some jobs will never serve the purpose of glorifying God. For instance, I wonder how people who claim to be

Christians can work in the tobacco industry. Knowing that each year cigarettes kill 450,000 Americans and more than 1.5 million people worldwide, it's hard for me to imagine how people who work in this industry can believe that they are living out vocational callings from God. I believe that there are some jobs that Christians should refuse to do. Quitting such jobs can be a Christian calling.

As the two of you think about your own vocational choices for the future, I want to suggest that you ask yourselves the following questions:

- Will this vocation enable me to best serve others as Christ would have me serve them?
- Will this vocation enable me to utilize the talents God has given me and actualize my potential as a creative person made in the image of the Ultimate Creator?
- Will this vocation provide me with emotional gratification, without which I will lack the energy to love others?
- Is this work environmentally responsible? Will I be contributing to the well-being of the planet?
- Will my work allow me to build community with coworkers, and will I be able to create a workplace in which love and justice can flourish?

Needless to say, it is very difficult to find work that allows you to answer all of these questions affirmatively.

But if you do not ask yourself these questions, and if you do not seek a vocation that allows you to realize the values implied in them, you are avoiding what God expects of you.

As you choose a vocation in which you will attempt great things for God, I encourage you to expect great things from God. With God all things are possible.

Sincerely,
Tony

20

■ Living Out the Great Commission

Dear Junia and Timothy,

We Evangelicals believe that the mission of the church *is* missions. Almost every Evangelical church has sent short-term mission teams to places of need. These mission teams build new schools and churches, conduct evangelistic outreach programs, and more. These days, it is unusual to get on a plane flying from Miami to Port-au-Prince, Haiti, and not find a mission team aboard. You will come across these short-term mission teams in almost every Third World country and, increasingly, in one-time Eastern Bloc nations such as Romania.

In almost every case, those who go on these trips are responsible for raising the money needed to cover their airfare and other expenses. Young people raise funds via car washes and bake sales, odd jobs, and, above all else, fundraising letters to family members and friends.

I would like you to consider participating in one of these short-term mission experiences. There is nothing like spending a couple of weeks among poor people in a Third World country to change your value system and deepen your commitment to Christ. It will help you realize how important it is for well-off churches in our country to build partnerships with impoverished Christians in places of need. Through such partnerships, we can work to empower them to expand their ministries to better meet the social and economic needs of their neighbors. Even a short time on the mission field will generate an intense desire to live out the Great Commission and minister to those in need.

While the Christians in many mainline churches often seem more inclined to carry out missionary work through their denominational bureaucracies, we Evangelicals generally want direct and personal involvement with the mission work we are supporting. Most Evangelicals want our churches to carry out our missionary concerns through personal connections with specific indigenous congregations on the mission field. We want face-to-face relationships with the people who will partner with us overseas in our missionary endeavors. We want to know the pastors and people of the churches we support.

All of this requires regular visits between our church people and the overseas Christians who partner with us in missionary work. These personal connections with churches on the mission field create emotional ties that lead U.S. Evangelicals to be extraordinarily generous in our missionary giving. Statistics show that Evangelicals give ten times as much money per capita to overseas mission work as do Christians in mainline churches.

Not only do Evangelicals give more money to missions on a per-capita basis, we also send far more of our people to mission fields as full-time workers than do mainline denominational churches. Most mainline denominations are cutting back on the number of missionaries stationed overseas because of declining contributions from member churches. At the same time, Evangelical missionary organizations—which generally require missionaries to raise their own financial support—have been growing exponentially. The highly Evangelical Youth With A Mission (YWAM) has more than 40,000 missionaries stationed around the world. In comparison, my own denomination, the American Baptist Churches, USA, has about 1.6 million members but only 110 full-time overseas missionaries. Operation Mobilisation, another Evangelical missionary organization, has 4,200 overseas missionaries, while the Presbyterian Church, USA, one of America's largest mainline denominations, has only 250 long-term mission workers.

When I first began teaching at Eastern University nearly four decades ago, I felt compelled to find a way to deploy young men and women from mainline churches who had been my students and felt called to do full-time missionary work. Most of these zealous young people found that their own denominations had no openings available for appointments. That is what led me to get together with some friends and establish the Evangelical Association for the Promotion of Education (EAPE). This independent missionary organization has created opportunities for hundreds of young people to do missionary work not only in Third World countries, but also in "at-risk" neighborhoods in nine different cities across North America.

If you are thinking about going to a Third World country on a short-term mission trip, let me recommend that you travel to Haiti, the poorest country in the western hemisphere, and visit some of the young people that EAPE has placed there. Just log on to *www.beyondborders.net* for details. A couple of my friends serving Christ in that desperate Caribbean nation will optimize the time you are able to give them.

What you will learn from the Haitians you meet there will blow your mind. You will visit a few of the many little schools they've developed for children known as *restaveks*. These are children whose families are so poor that they have sent their children away to live with families whose economic situation is slightly better. Parents do this in hopes that their children might get better care and perhaps a better education than they would at home. In most cases, these families are deceived, and their children end up being exploited in ways that reduce them to little more than slaves. The brokers who make the placement arrangements for these children are well aware that the families that take them in have in mind securing house servants and have no intention of spending the money required to send them to school.

In trying to help the more than 300,000 *restaveks* in Haiti, the folks at our EAPE-related ministry, Beyond Borders, have established small village schools. The classes in these little schools are held in the late afternoons and evenings so that the *restaveks* can attend after their housework is done. When you visit a couple of those schools, meet the students and their teachers, see their desperate needs, and feel the gratitude the children readily express for the chance to learn how to read and write, you will be deeply moved. You probably will end up wanting to finance one of these schools, each of which has between thirty and fifty students. The cost of running a school is only $200 a month, which primarily pays a salary to an indigenous teacher that is twice the going rate for such teachers in Haiti. You two can probably come up with that kind of money—and once you see the hope and joy these schools offer to the *restaveks*, I'm sure you will want to.

Responding to poverty and oppression in personal and direct ways such as supporting a school for *restaveks* is wonderful. But the problem with many Christian charity efforts is that they leave the political and economic arrangements that create poverty and oppression unchallenged. That's why Beyond Borders not only offers help and support to *restavek* children, but also is active in the campaign to end the practice of child servitude throughout Haiti.

We Evangelicals have a long history of effective charity work in the Third World, but there is a growing sense among socially progressive Evangelicals that something must be done to change the social system itself. This awareness, in most cases, is driving such Evangelicals to become increasingly sympathetic with those indigenous people in the Third World who challenge the legitimacy of not only their own government and business leaders but also America's policies in the Third World. Increasingly, U.S. Evangelicals return from mission trips asking whether our government in Washington has established trade agreements that serve our nation's commercial interests to the detriment of developing nations such as Haiti.

I am one of those questioning Evangelicals. I think it is our Christian responsibility to ask if the U.S. government has lent support to violent, dictatorial regimes simply because those regimes are friendly to our multinational corporations. It doesn't take too much investigating to discover that our country maintains the School of the Americas, which knowingly trains military officers from

Third World countries that too often suppress, with violence, dissident voices in their homelands. Missionary involvement can lead us to sympathize with and advocate for those who seek to get rid of such agents of oppression. Missionary work usually starts as acts of charity, but the more you learn about how political and economic institutions oppress and exploit the poor, the more you realize that charity is not enough. Justice is also needed.

Many socially progressive young Evangelicals in today's world sadly recognize that the church has, time and time again over its history, sided with oppressors—and that, far too often, it still does. They know about the 1960s, when many white church leaders, particularly in the South, stood in opposition to Martin Luther King Jr. and the goals of the civil-rights movement. They've groaned in disdain to tales of leading religious leaders who sought to religiously legitimate the Vietnam War. More recently, they've been dismayed to witness TV preachers giving their blessings to the war in Iraq and supporting a government that establishes secret prisons where people are tortured. These young Evangelicals often express disgust at "Christian" radio shows that nurture homophobia by equating homosexuality with pedophilia and encouraging Christians to crusade for the denial of basic civil rights to gays and lesbians. Those with ecological concerns recognize that, in their efforts to save the environment, their primary opponents are often Evangelical Christians. They wince as Evangelical preachers, writers, and radio commentators label Christian environmentalists as nothing more than a bunch of "New Agers."

Unfortunately, many of these questioning Evangelicals have ended up rejecting the church. A young former Evangelical Christian I know, who has committed her life to social-justice causes, believes that when it comes to the sicknesses of the world, religion is not the cure. Instead, she says, it's often a perpetrator of the disease. She echoes those who call religion "the opiate of the people" and views religion as an instrument that powerful people use to dupe oppressed people into believing that the prevailing unjust social arrangements are ordained by God. Now alienated from the church, she is especially upset when Evangelical leaders suggest that, if people rebel against what she believes are obscenely unfair social institutions, they are actually rebelling against God. She is fed up with Bible-pounding preachers who press this point by reading to their people Romans 13:1–2, which says,

> *Let every soul be subject unto the higher powers. For there is no power but of God: the powers that be are ordained of God. Whosoever therefore resisteth the power, resisteth the ordinance of God: and they that resist shall receive to themselves damnation.*

This young, idealistic activist is well aware that whenever ruling authorities are challenged and revolution is in the air, conservative church leaders are apt to remind people of Paul's teachings in these verses. Consequently, she does not find it surprising that just about every revolution, including the American Revolution, was condemned by most leaders of "established" churches as being contrary to the will of God. She sides with leftist radicals who note that that the highest church officials in Latin America have often stood side by side on palace balconies with totalitarian tyrants, offering religious legitimation to their unjust rule.

Fortunately, under the influence of progressive Evangelical writers and speakers such as John Perkins, Ron Sider, and Jim Wallis, a growing number of our churches have been sensitized to justice concerns and are actively engaged in trying to deal with social evils. Sadly, my justice-minded young friend has not been a part of such a church. Her own church effectively shut her off from progressive Evangelical social thought, making sure that she attended a Bible college that treated social-justice concerns as a leftist substitute for the real mission of the church.

Consequently, this dedicated young woman did not learn that the Bible is *not* about legitimating oppressive regimes. It is really the story of a liberating God. From the book of Exodus, which tells of the deliverance of the Jews from enslavement, to Jesus's identification with the poor and oppressed, the Bible is an account of a God who calls for justice and equality. I hope that you come to see the God revealed in the Bible this way. The God of Scripture wills the creation of a new social order in which poverty, economic injustice, environmental degradation, and the many fears that plague most peoples of the earth are no more.

The wrong use of religion, as seen by my activist friend, must be challenged—in the Third World and everywhere else. It is true that religion can be used as an instrument of oppression, but contrariwise, it can provide divine imperatives that give authority to the quest for justice. Furthermore, such imperatives can be found in the Bible. I hope it's not too late to convince young people like my socially concerned friend that there are many Evangelical churches that can provide encouragement and support for their hopes for a more just society. Many of our churches have shaken off the Fundamentalist anti–social Gospel mentality and are intensely involved in promoting progressive social change. Increasingly, Evangelicals are learning to be social activists.

Much of what we are learning about social activism is being taught to us by people in the Third World. In Latin America, there are Catholic Christians who are finding the authority to challenge unjust regimes as they read the Bible in spiritually charged groups known as base communities. These are small gatherings of Christians brought together and nurtured by priests and nuns while studying the Bible, have found the inspiration and courage to challenge the injustices that plague their lives and their communities. For years, many U.S. Evangelicals were reluctant to lend any credence to the insights coming out of base communities, not only because they had Marxist overtones, but also because of an Evangelical antipathy to anything Roman Catholic. But that is changing both because there is a growing Evangelical movement within Catholicism and because many Evangelicals, in their efforts to develop disciplines that will deepen their prayer life, are learning much from the insights of Catholic mystics such as Ignatius of Loyola and Francis of Assisi. Given this growing rapprochement between Catholics and Evangelicals, it is not surprising that progressives in our camp are willing to give consideration to the truths emerging out of Catholic base communities.

I first encountered base communities more than thirty years ago when I took some of my students on a short-term mission trip. During the mission, we went to a despicable slum area located on the edge of Santo Domingo in the Dominican Republic. While there, we attended a morning Mass at a Catholic church led by a priest whom I greatly admired because of the incredible good he was doing for the people living in that barrio. His compassion for the needy seemed to have no limits, and his entrepreneurial skills had enabled him to establish economic-development programs, clinics, and schools in that slum.

The morning of our visit, the church was packed. My students and I stood against the back wall as we watched the Mass unfold. So many people had gathered for the service that there were at least one hundred parishioners outside the church building, pressed against the open windows, hoping to hear what was going on inside.

The reason for the huge turnout was that the priest was going to report to the people about his negotiations with government officials. Their barrio, which was located on the edge of the river leading from the sea into Santo Domingo, had been slated to be bulldozed to make way for a marina where rich tourists from the United States could park their yachts. This meant that thousands of people who lived in this slum would lose the shacks they lived in and have no place to go. Each Thursday, the priest met with government leaders at the presidential palace in hopes of persuading them to either forego their plans to destroy this barrio or, better still, provide the people with a new and decent place to live.

Before the priest had finished reporting on his progress, a young man in the congregation stood up and yelled, "But, Father, what if all this talk comes to nothing? What if these negotiations lead nowhere, and they come to destroy our homes? What will we do when they come with bulldozers to level all our shacks?"

The priest had no chance to answer before another young man, this one on the other side of the cinder-block church, stood and yelled, "If they come with bull-dozers to destroy our homes, we will fight them." Then he shouted even louder, "We will fight them to the death!" Calling out to the congregation, he chanted, "Are you with me? Are you with me?"

The congregation yelled back, "Yes! Yes! Yes! We are with you!"

Then, in the midst of this uproar, the priest raised his arms and yelled at the top of his lungs, "SILENCE!" Turning to the altar, he lifted up the bread and the wine, which to him and the people gathered together in the church that Sunday morning were the body and blood of Christ. He then cried out, "When they come with bull-dozers to destroy our homes, and we go out to fight them, *he* will be with us, too!"

After that incredible morning, my Evangelical students and I had a long discussion about all that we'd seen and heard. Although we concluded that the violent de-struction of those who do evil is not Jesus's way, there was no question in our minds that in the struggle for justice, God sides with the poor and oppressed against the strong and the powerful. For the first time, these students un-derstood liberation theology, and they supported it—if by "liberation theology" we mean the declaration that, in the struggle to end injustice, God sides with the poor and oppressed against their oppressors.

Mother Teresa believed that there is a unique spirituality that comes to us through the poor. She claimed that this is what Jesus was talking about when he told us that in ministering to the poor, we find his presence (Matthew 25). Saint Francis said much the same thing. Regardless of the source of this truth, there is little doubt that poor and downtrodden people experience God in a special way; through them, we can experience a profound revelation from God. Through fellowship with the poor, we learn things about God that can be learned no other way.

Not too long ago, I was a guest speaker at a prominent theological seminary. I told the students about a study that had analyzed all kinds of religious people, from Franciscan monks to Baptist evangelists. This study had determined that the most spiritual people in America were African American grandmothers who lived along the border between Alabama and Georgia. Most of these women had little more than a grade-school education, lived well below the poverty line, and were trying to raise grandchildren who had been abandoned by their parents. I asked the students if they were surprised to learn that these old women, struggling to survive at a subsistence level while rearing young children, were the Americans who were most into prayer, reading the Bible, and evidencing "the fruit of the Spirit" described in Galatians 5:22–23. I wanted to know whether they were amazed to find that these impoverished grandmothers, with more burdens than most of us could handle, were the people of our country who were most likely to show love, joy, meekness, peace of mind, long-suffering, gentleness, goodness, and faith. With one voice, the students answered, "No!"

I had them set up for my next question, which was admittedly somewhat tongue-in-cheek: "If these grandmothers living in poverty down South are the most spiritual people in America, if it is with them that you are most likely to experience the presence of Christ, then why are you studying with scholars up here at this seminary?"

This elicited some smiles, but there was no way that the students could deny that these simple elderly folks might offer a more profound revelation of Christ than the seminary academicians with all of their erudition. For those who worship scholarly credentials, it is hard to consider the idea that untrained and unsophisticated people might be the ones through whom Christ chooses to reveal himself and show us the essence of being Christian. This may be difficult for proud intellectuals to accept, but it echoes Paul's statement that God chooses to reveal truth through those whom the world calls "nobodies," so as to humble the proud who trust in their learning instead of trusting in God (1 Corinthians 1:26–31).

Christians who travel to Third World countries usually return with reports of how they were blessed as they worshipped among the poor. Their testimonies often echo the words of one of my former students, who claimed he'd had a kind of "second born-again experience" during a Sunday-evening prayer service among the poor in a Haitian church in a place called Cité Soleil. He said,

> *There's no way of describing the scene. The poverty outside that cinder-block church building left me totally unprepared for what I experienced inside. Outside was a slum marked by sights and odors that were more than disgusting. Yet inside the church, there was an aliveness among the people unmatched by anything I had ever known before. I soaked in the Holy Spirit that enveloped me—and I've never been the same since. I saw Jesus in their faces.*

No wonder Jesus commanded the rich young ruler in Mark 10 to sell all he had and give it to the poor if he wanted to experience the fullness of God and inherit eternal life. It was not just that the poor needed help. Jesus knew what would happen to that young man when he encountered the poor. The poor are in touch with spiritual realities that self-sufficient rich folks can never know, and they can reveal much about Jesus. That is why going to the Third World, even for a short-term mission trip, is a very important thing for you to do.

When we listen to the poor, the Holy Spirit can teach us a great many things about the Scriptures that middle-class people like me often fail to grasp. I got an inkling of this when a black man from a poor neighborhood came to speak at my predominantly white university. He started off by saying, "The first thing that you must understand about Jesus is that Jesus was a nigger!"

Shock waves ran through the audience. He then explained, "When I tell you that Jesus was a nigger, I don't mean that he had black skin. There are some black folks who call other black folks niggers. What they mean when they call those folks niggers is that they think those folks are trash. That's what I mean when I say Jesus was a nigger. Listen to what the Bible says about him in Isaiah, in the 53rd chapter, and then try to tell me he wasn't a nigger."

As we sat stunned, he proceeded to read some verses from Isaiah 53:

For he shall grow up before him a tender plant, and as a root out of a dry ground: he hath no form nor comeliness; and when we shall see him, there is no beauty that we should desire him. He is despised and rejected of men; a man of sorrows, and acquainted

> with grief: and we hid as it were our faces from him;
> he was despised, and we esteemed him not. . . . He was
> oppressed, and he was afflicted, yet he opened not his
> mouth: he is brought as a lamb to the slaughter and as
> a sheep before her shearers is dumb, so he openeth not
> his mouth.

"If you think that prophet was talking about our Jesus," the speaker said, "then Jesus was a nigger." As if that wasn't enough, he went on to say that not only was Jesus a nigger, but he came with a message that only niggers could really understand. "So if you want to understand what the Bible is saying," he continued, "then you've got to read the Bible like a nigger does!"

I am not sure how many people bought into that preacher's message, but he certainly shook up the college-chapel crowd that day and sent us all away thinking. He had declared, in no uncertain terms, that the Bible has to be read through the eyes of the poor and oppressed because it is primarily the story of a God who hears the cries of those who are oppressed, both spiritually and socially, and offers them deliverance. He had made it clear that to limit the salvation story to spiritual deliverance alone, as affluent white folks are prone to do, is to fail to tell the whole salvation story.

Deliverance from social and economic oppression must also be part of the Gospel story. In this speaker's reading of the Bible, God provides deliverance not only from sin and guilt, but also from poverty and racial discrimination.

If you think this sounds awfully radical, I can only respond by saying that what Jesus preached 2,000 years ago also was radical. Dietrich Bonhoeffer, a German theologian and Christian author, once said, "When Jesus calls a man, he calls him to come and die." By that, Bonhoeffer meant that the kind of commitment Jesus expects of those who would call themselves his disciples requires the death of personal and nationalistic self-interests, the sacrifice of material possessions and ego in response to the needs of the impoverished, beaten-down people of the world. Privileged Christians are called to be the voices for those who have no voice and to identify with those whom the world calls niggers. Living and serving among the poor will transform you into persons who will want to be radical for Jesus and his people.

You don't even have to travel outside our country to experience the Third World. It's right here waiting for you in most American cities. The conditions of poverty and despair so evident in the Third World are emerging on the derelict streets of our own urban neighborhoods. That's why EAPE also has developed inner-city ministries.

If you don't go overseas, consider spending a couple of weeks with our Urban Promise program in Camden, New Jersey. *Time* magazine calls Camden the worst city in the nation. Ninety-two percent of the babies born in that city in 2005 were born out of wedlock. One out of every seven of its houses has been abandoned. More than 10,000 people drive into this city of 80,000 each day to buy drugs. The full-time unemployment rate is sometimes as high as thirty percent. Almost thirty percent of those who live in Camden live below the poverty level. I know that the place sounds like hell—but if you spend a couple of weeks working there in one of our summer or after-school programs, you'll meet the kids who live there, and they are likely to steal your hearts.

Let me warn you, however, that among the poor in Camden, you'll probably experience the same kind of consciousness raising that my student experienced in that Dominican barrio. I believe that something mystical will transpire in your soul. By the time those poor people finish with you, you won't be able to read the Bible the same way. As you listen to the people who live there, the Holy Spirit will teach you things about Scripture that you'd never learn from scholarly exegesis.

In sociology there is a concept called "praxis." The central idea is that reflection in the context of action transforms our minds in ways that pure intellectual reflection cannot. In doing missionary work, you will discover that this is true. As you reflect in both mind and spirit, and actively engage in bringing the Gospel to the lost, meeting the needs of the poor, and entering into struggles for social justice, you will develop new ways of thinking. It is likely that your worldview will change. You will probably come out thinking a lot more like that priest in the Dominican Republic and that African American preacher at my university than you might predict. I am convinced that God will teach you more through those whom you serve than you will ever teach them.

We all have a lot to learn from those whom, as the Bible says, "the world calls nothing" (I Cor. 26–28). The way to begin that learning is to be among them for a while.

Sincerely,
Tony

21

▪ The Need for Feedback from the Twilight Zone

Dear Timothy and Junia,

I've shared with you my thoughts about Evangelicalism in my letters about our church's history and politics. I've explained what we Evangelicals believe and discussed the issues that concern us today. But now it's your turn. I'd like to know what you think about the future of the Evangelical movement. Given that you and other young people will be shaping Evangelicalism in the twenty-first century, I'm wondering what you think will happen to our movement in the years that lie ahead.

Many sociologists speculate that within the next few years there may be a reaction to Evangelicalism that will pull massive numbers of our people away from our churches. They suggest that the close alliance that Evangelicalism has had with conservative politics may be our undoing. During the '50s and early '60s mainline denominations tended to be connected with the politics of the left, and when the pendulum swung in a conservative direction many Americans left those churches. Do you think that the political pendulum might swing back in a liberal direction leaving Evangelicals high and dry because of their marriage to the Republican party?

I'd like to know what you think our churches will look like in the future. Our people have been strongly attracted to mega-churches such as the famous Willow Creek Community Church in Barrington, Illinois, with its 25,000 members. That church has become a model that is being replicated all across the country. Do you think that, as a consequence of this, churches with just a few hundred members will fade toward oblivion? We all know that they can't compete with the mega-churches when it comes to programming. Mega-churches have specialized ministries for every age group, with expert leadership in each of them. Organizationally, mega-churches are superior to the smaller churches that have long characterized American Christianity. Mega-churches even have specialized, small-group ministries that offer the intimate fellowship that people often seek and need.

While considering all the positives of megachurches you must not ignore the fact that while serving the personal needs of their people, megachurches seldom have preachers who take the risks that go with being socially prophetic. The preachers are not likely to raise questions about the militarism, sexism, homophobia, and the

hypernationalism that often pervades their congregations. Usually it is the smaller mainline churches that take
on such issues and run into trouble with their people.

Demographic studies of mainline denominational
congregations show that their people are mostly elderly, and it is only a matter of time before they'll be
gone. As the elderly move from the nave to the grave,
these denominations are not adding new members at
anything like an equivalent rate. Perhaps the most serious problem faced by mainline denominational churches
is that they have largely lost the capacity to do the kind
of evangelism that is essential for their survival. I'm referring to the kind of evangelism that has become the
hallmark of Evangelicalism and that brings new members into churches. Given these realities do you think
that smaller mainline denominations could fade into
insignificance?

I'd also love to hear your thoughts on why so many
young people who remain Evangelical in their convictions are nonetheless dropping out of organized religion. There seems to be a religion-less Evangelicalism
emerging, wherein more and more young people are
into being spiritual while disengaging from church
membership. They read religious books and pray but
find churches boring and irrelevant. Many of them are
offended by the ways in which their gay and lesbian
friends are treated by Evangelical churches and react
negatively to sermons that relegate their non-Christian

friends to Hell. These religiously disengaged Evangelicals seem to want intimacy with God, but they contend that this intimacy is not something that they were able to experience within organized religion. Do you think that we'll be seeing more of their kind in the future? Do you think that their spirituality is a valid form of Christianity?

I'm also very curious about your sense of the morality of your generation. I have a hard time accepting that so many unmarried Evangelical couples are living together and that many young Evangelicals view premarital sex as no big deal. Is the old moral code that we older people believe was dictated by Scripture passé? What are we older folks to make of all this?

What do you think about the future roles of women within Evangelicalism? Already the Southern Baptist Convention has rescinded the ordination of women, and several Evangelical Presbyterian denominations are considering doing the same. How do you think Evangelical young people will react to what many of your generation deem reactionary attitudes toward women?

Then there's the matter of the crises that loom on the horizon. What will be the outcome of the AIDS crisis? Bono, the rock musician, has said that how we respond to this crisis will determine how we Christians will be viewed in the next century. How do you think you and your peers will grapple with this plague in the years to come?

There's also the rising specter of an all-out war between the Islamic world and what might be called the Christianized West. Do you think that we might be facing a new era of wars that will be even more devastating than the Crusades? What role do you think Evangelicals should play in what Americans are currently calling a war on terrorism?

Then there's the matter of technology. Already we Evangelicals are suffering from "future shock." There is just so much to think about. For instance, what are the moral implications of test-tube babies? How are we to think about euthanasia now that we are able to keep a brain-dead person alive indefinitely?

And what about genome research? The genetic makeup of humans has been decoded. Francis Collins, who headed up the government's genome project, has said that this has been the most significant scientific advance since Isaac Newton's discovery of the laws of motion. Soon we will be able to genetically engineer the elimination of physical disabilities and most diseases. We now have access to the aging gene. Does that mean that it's only a matter of time before we can maintain a person's life indefinitely? And what are the theological implications of all of this?

A friend of mine at Harvard University told me that, in a rudimentary way, scientists have been able to program the electronic waves of the brain onto a computer disk. "What if," he asked, "they are able to replicate every organ of your body and technologically reproduce your brain? Will the creature that they create really be you—or is there more to who you are than that?" This is an incredibly complicated theological question—and one that you are likely to confront in the course of your lifetime.

Soon, we will probably have the technology to reproduce mystical spiritual experiences by stimulating certain parts of the brain. What if the kinds of spiritual ecstasies experienced by St. Francis in the chapel of San Damiano or John Wesley at the Aldersgate chapel become available through scientific means? Such questions may seem strange now, but your generation will have to cope with technological possibilities that are beyond my generation's comprehension. You will need to be prepared, ethically and theologically, to answer them.

I can tell you something of where Evangelicalism has come from and what it is in our present day, but you young Evangelicals will have to determine its place in the brave new world that lies ahead. The future will present awesome challenges, and I hope and pray that you will be up to meeting them. Right now, I can only hope for the best while I wait for you to answer the questions that I have posed as well as even more essential and complex questions that I cannot even formulate.

Needless to say, I wait with bated breath to learn of your answers to questions about the future. I've told you the little that I know about the past and present of Evangelicalism, but both you and I know that the future is yours to create.

Sincerely,
Tony